The New Americans
Recent Immigration and American Society

Edited by
Carola Suárez-Orozco and Marcelo Suárez-Orozco

A Series from LFB Scholarly

Bridges and Barriers
Earnings and Occupational Attainment among Immigrants

Jennifer Karas

LFB Scholarly Publishing LLC
New York 2002

Library of Congress Cataloging-in-Publication Data

Karas, Jennifer.
   Bridges and barriers : earnings and occupational attainment among immigrants / Jennifer Karas.
      p. cm. -- (The new Americans : recent immigration and American society)
   Includes bibliographical references and index.
   ISBN 1-931202-16-8
   1. Alien labor--United States. 2. Immigrants--United States--Economic conditions. I. Title. II. New Americans (LFB Scholarly Publishing LLC)
   HD8081.A5 K37 2002
   331.6'2'0973--dc21

2001005908

ISBN 1-931202-16-8

Printed on acid-free 250-year-life paper.

Manufactured in the United States of America.

To Todd and Caroline with love

Contents

List of Tables

List of Figures

Acknowledgements

There are many individuals who contributed to the completion of this project and to whom I am grateful. I am greatly indebted to Henry A. Walker for his guidance with an earlier version of this book. His pragmatic approach, grueling drive for perfection, relentless critiques, and unfailing patience have pushed me to become a better writer, and, I hope, a better sociologist. He has helped me remember how much I enjoy research, and for that I am truly thankful. Ronald Breiger and Phyllis Moen also provided critical feedback that helped me improve the clarity and precision of my work. The Cornell Institute for Social and Economic Research was a wonderful source of information and support. Thank you to the CISER staff, especially Resa Alvord, Ann Gray, and Mary-Elizabeth Vault for providing me with data assistance and guidance on many (desperate) occasions. The original data analysis was supported with funds from the College of Arts and Sciences at Cornell University.

I would also like to acknowledge the support of Gregg Kvistad, Dean of Arts, Humanities, and Social Sciences at the University of Denver for allowing me the time to research and to write. His encouragement has helped me maintain a much desired connection to research in my current administrative post.

My Mom, as always, has been a terrific cheerleader. My sister, Michelle Karas, was a wonderful critic and proofreader. Many thanks for her careful attention to detail. Any mistakes that may remain are, of course, my fault entirely. Caroline Karas Myers and her sibling-to-be have been much needed distractions for me. Thank you for filling my life with love and kisses. Finally, I thank my husband, Todd Myers, for reading far too many drafts of this book, his many insights on immigration and the American political economy, for being my roadie, but most of all for his constant love and support. ILY.

CHAPTER 1

Introduction and Overview

INTRODUCTION

New waves of immigration are again transforming the United States and in the process creating a new racial and cultural mosaic. Yet, while the increased immigration set off by the 1965 immigration policy reforms continues America's immigrant heritage, changes both in the origin of the newcomers and in the economy have created a new and more varied immigration experience. The experiences of the newest arrivals provide unique opportunities to explore ethnic stratification issues within the U.S. Accordingly, the paths immigrants take toward social and economic assimilation reveal as much about how they ultimately will fare in society as they do about the future of race and ethnic stratification. The social and economic attainments of recent immigrants from Asia and Latin America suggest that ethnic and racial stratification may persist well into the 21st century. Variation in human and social capital and in the characteristics of the local labor markets immigrants enter, in addition to discrimination, may be important correlates of contemporary ethnic stratification. To that end, this research describes ethnic differences in social and economic attainments among recent immigrants and examines social and economic explanations for such differences.

A Nation of Immigrants

As a nation of immigrants, the U.S. has historically drawn millions of people from across the world who seek a new life. Immigration has in turn transformed the cultural and social landscape of the U.S. throughout its history. Immigration during the 17th and 18th centuries created a dominant European presence in America and brought African slaves to the emerging country. Later waves of immigrants in the 19th and early 20th centuries solidified the European hold on the emerging culture and introduced smaller groups of Asians to the western U.S. Despite the fact that the majority of immigrants were from Europe, perceived cultural and economic differences created conflict between immigrants and the native-born population.

The large scale immigration in the late 19th and early 20th centuries fueled U.S. industrialization and the growing economy. The low wage needs of metropolitan areas were continually replenished by successive waves of immigration, which ensured a supply of cheap laborers. Relying on their physical strength as their greatest asset, these immigrants found work in heavy industry and small-scale agriculture. Because cities were the centers of low skill employment, most immigrants sought employment there.

Contemporary immigrants share certain similarities with the immigrants who came before them, but overall experience a different reception in the U.S. for several reasons. The newest immigrants are predominantly Latin American or Asian, and thus have different cultures, races, languages, and skill sets than the immigrants of the past or the contemporary native-born population. The conditions they encounter in the U.S. have also changed. Earlier immigrants faced a geographically expanding U.S. with a strong industrial and manufacturing economy and a growing population. In contrast, immigrants today encounter a shrinking low skill job sector and a growing service economy with demands for technically skilled workers.

Initiated by the immigration reforms of 1965, new waves of Asian and Latin American immigrants have entered the U.S. in large numbers. In the decades since, shifts in technology, manufacturing, and the growth of the service sector have radically altered the demands on the U.S. labor supply. The rapid pace of technological transformation, the decline of international trade barriers, and the rate of consumer spending have dramatically reshaped employment patterns for both native-born and foreign-born workers alike. The experiences of contemporary immigrants to the U.S. reflect these changes.

As a response to their Third World origins, the popular conception of the newcomers is that they are poor and unskilled. These immigrants are actually split between those who are highly skilled and well educated and those who have minimal skills or training. Highly skilled immigrants do not seek employment in the lowest tier of jobs and are thus more evenly distributed throughout the economy than the industrial immigrants of the early twentieth century. Many have advanced educational degrees and a wealth of business experience, which may facilitate their economic and social assimilation into the U.S. Those with less training and fewer skills continue to rely on employment in low technology and menial service industries located in large urban centers. These immigrants present a continuity with past immigrants who also lacked skills, education, familiarity with English, and who faced high levels of discrimination from the native-born population. Yet the varied industrial and manufacturing jobs that earlier immigrants relied upon for employment are now much fewer in number. In their place are low wage jobs in the service sector--many of which do not provide adequate stability or compensation to support a family. For this group, the center city has become a center of poverty, rather than the center of economic possibility that it once was.

The Changing Face of America

The influence of the latest groups of foreign-born on contemporary population trends is significant. After the 1965 immigration law went into effect, Latin America and Asia replaced Europe as the largest sources of immigration. This trend has grown tremendously over time, so that by the 1990s, Asian and Hispanic immigrants make up more than 80% of new arrivals as compared to less than 20% during the 1940s, as shown in Table 1.1.

Immigration continues to have a significant influence on the population growth of the U.S., given that immigrants accounted for almost 30% of the total growth from 1980 to 1990. This type of population growth based on immigration has not always been the case. Immigrants actually became a declining proportion of the total U.S. population after the passage of the Emergency National Origin Quota Act of 1921. Recent increases in the number of immigrants have reversed this trend. As shown in Table 1.1 from 1911-1920 immigrants 14.7% of the total population. From this high level, the proportion of foreign-born dropped steadily until it reached 4.8% from 1961-1970.

Table 1.1: Foreign-born as a Percentage of the U.S. Population

Decade	Total Number	% of Population	% Change due to Immigration	% from NW Europe	% from SE Europe	% from Asia	% from Latin America
1820-1830	151,824	10.4	4.1	67.9	2.2	-	6.2
1831-1840	599,125	9.3	13.2	81.7	1.0	-	3.3
1841-1850	1,713,251	9.7	24.5	92.9	0.3	-	1.2
1851-1860	2,598,214	13.2	33.4	93.6	0.8	1.6	0.6
1861-1870	2,314,824	14.0	25.6	88.1	1.1	2.8	0.5
1871-1880	2,812,191	13.3	26.7	76.2	4.5	4.4	0.7
1881-1890	5,246,613	14.7	41.0	78.8	11.5	1.3	0.6
1891-1900	3,687,564	13.6	28.3	60.6	35.8	2.0	1.0
1901-1910	8,795,386	14.7	52.3	46.1	45.5	3.7	2.1
1911-1920	5,735,811	13.2	45.1	25.3	49.9	4.3	7.0
1921-1930	4,107,209	11.6	24.9	32.5	27.0	2.7	14.4
1931-1940	528,431	8.8	7.4	38.6	26.7	3.0	9.7
1941-1950	1,035,039	6.9	4.6	49.9	9.8	3.1	14.9
1951-1960	2,515,479	5.4	8.9	39.7	12.7	6.1	22.2
1961-1970	3,321,677	4.8	13.5	18.3	15.4	12.9	38.6
1971-1980	4,493,314	6.2	18.8	6.7	11.0	35.3	40.3
1981-1990	7,338,000	7.9	29.7	7.2	5.3	37.3	47.1

Sources: Leon F. Bouvier and Robert Gardner, "Immigration to the U.S.: The Unfinished Story." Population Bulletin, (1986). Statistical Abstracts of the United Sates 1995, 1990 Census of Population The Foreign-born Population in the United States CP-3-1, Roger Daniels Coming to America 1990, and Steve H Murdock (1995) An America Challenged: Population Change and the Future of the United States.

Currently, the proportion of immigrants in the total U.S. population is again rising; immigrants now make up over 7.9% of the total.[1]

Although rising birth levels historically have been the major source of population expansion, net immigration has become increasingly important to the recent growth of the nation. Minority populations are not only growing more rapidly than the white populations, but also are increasing as a proportion of the total population, which may be due in part to the decline in white fertility (Murdock 1995). The total fertility rate for native-born women is now less than replacement, estimated at 1.8 births per lifetime (Fosler et al 1990), while foreign-born women have a total fertility rate of 2.7 births per lifetime per woman (Bouvier and Grant 1994). From 1980 to 1990, the white population increased by 5.6%, the Black population increased by 13.2%, other racial categories (Asian and Pacific Islanders, American Indians, Eskimos and other groups) increased by 72.6%, and Hispanics increased by 53.1% (Fosler et al 1990). This trend supports the assertion that the future growth of the U.S. population will in large part be due to immigrants and their descendants. This expanding section of the population raises public concern because of the marked differences in the social and economic attainment of immigrant groups, even among groups that share similar cultural characteristics.

Ethnic Variation in Attainment

The diversity of origins, skills, and resources that the new immigrants possess, combined with their reception into the U.S., send them into different pathways toward social and economic assimilation. Traditionally, the individuals who fare the best in terms of median income and educational attainment are native-born non-Hispanic whites. This group, descendants of European immigrants themselves, frequently comprises the standard population in the U.S. to which the achievements of other groups, including contemporary immigrants, are evaluated. This study utilizes foreign-born non-Hispanic whites as the

---

[1]The figures in Table 1.1 reflect the fact that large numbers of foreign-born are not always counted. African slaves, who formed 19% of the U.S. population in 1790, may not have been included in either the native-born or foreign-born categories. Furthermore, these figures do not include estimates of illegal immigration.

reference population for five non-white immigrant groups. Presumably over time, this cluster of individuals drawn primarily from European ethnic groups will integrate most rapidly into the existing occupational structure of the U.S., since they resemble most closely the mainstream native-born population. Therefore this group represents a logical comparison for the non-white foreign-born groups in this sample.

The newest immigrants vary substantially in how they fare economically and socially in the U.S. Some immigrants arrive with differing levels of education, skills, and economic capital than others, levels that may be different than other members of their ethnic group already living in the U.S. This may leave them either at a disadvantage economically, or poised to reap the benefits of their position. As shown in Table 1.2, the majority of the newest immigrants are less educated than native-born U.S. citizens. However, there is growing evidence of an immigrant elite with advanced degrees, professional or business skills, and English language facility, all of which may lower the cost of migration to the U.S. Some evidence suggests that once established, these immigrant elite rapidly gain local status and business connections in order to achieve economically. The number of foreign-born government officials, business leaders, and researchers attest to this growing phenomenon. In fact, the proportion of immigrants who are managers and professionals exceeds the average for native-born workers (Portes and Rumbaut 1996).

Nevertheless, compared to the economic status of the native-born population, immigrants as a whole have not fared as well. It generally takes time for immigrants to translate foreign skills into a new work environment, to learn the language, to access business networks necessary to effectively compete in a new working arena, and to overcome the cost of ethnic and racial discrimination. These costs to immigration are reflected in the lower household income of many groups as compared to the native-born white population in Table 1.2. The fact that the median household income for all groups except Filipino immigrants is lower than that for the native-born population, and that some groups have levels similar to African Americans raises questions about racial and ethnic differences in the processes that influence income and other status attainment.

While some groups have been able to reach income parity with white native-born workers over time, others lag behind. This variation in social and economic attainment seems not to depend wholly on a

Table 1.2: Social and Economic Characteristics of Selected Foreign-born and Native-born Groups 1990

Place of Birth	% Entered 1980-90	% over 65	High School Graduates	College Graduates	% in Professional Jobs	% in Labor Jobs	Median Household Income (1989 $)
Foreign-born	43.8	13.6	58.8	20.4	12.3	18.6	28,314
Europe	17.9	31.4	63.5	18.0	15.4	12.8	30,892
Cambodia	85.8	3.4	35.4	5.5	5.5	29.2	19,728
China	53.5	17.9	60.6	30.9	16.9	16.1	30,597
Korea	56.1	5.3	80.1	34.4	13.3	13.0	30,147
Philippines	49.0	10.4	82.5	43.0	18.0	10.7	45,419
Vietnam	61.8	3.3	58.9	15.9	10.7	29.8	30,039
Mexico	49.9	4.9	24.3	3.5	2.6	32.2	21,926
Cuba	25.5	21.1	54.1	15.6	10.9	18.0	27,292
Dom. Republic	53.1	5.0	41.7	7.5	5.2	31.0	19,996
Africa	59.3	4.1	87.9	47.1	22.1	11.7	30,907
Native-born[a]							
White	n/a	12.8	79.1	22.0	27.9	13.7[b]	35,975
Black	n/a	8.2	66.2	11.3	18.1	20.8[b]	20,209

Sources: *Statistical Abstracts of the United States 1995* and *1990 Census of Population Social and Economic Characteristics of the United States CP 2-1.*

[a] Both categories include individuals of Hispanic descent.
[b] Includes operatives and laborers.

well-established immigrant history in the U.S. For example, large numbers of Mexicans have lived in areas of the continental U.S. for centuries. However, their median household income is among the lowest of those displayed in Table 1.2. These data suggest that they have not established an elite economic tradition upon which contemporary Mexican immigrants can build. In comparison, Filipino immigrants, whose presence in the U.S. has grown substantially only in the past two decades, far surpass native-born whites in terms of average household income and percent of population with college degrees.

In apparent contrast to the experience of some groups, length of residence does have a profound influence on social and economic attainments of individual immigrants. Longer amounts of time spent adjusting to the new social and economic environment can result in dramatic differences in attainment. As shown in Table 1.3, immigrants who arrived in the U.S. prior to 1980 have much higher household incomes, lower rates of family poverty, lower levels of linguistic isolation, and higher educational attainment than those who came after 1980. For example, Koreans who arrived in the U.S. prior to 1980 report an average household income of $44,358, while those who arrived after 1980 report an average household income of $25,516. Additionally, Cambodians who settled in the U.S. prior to 1980 report 19.7% of families living below the poverty line, while that figure rises to 46.6% for families who arrive later.

Strategies for Studying Ethnic Differences

In examining ethnic variation in immigrant assimilation, previous analyses have focused either on characteristics of immigrants, or on ecological considerations separately. My research integrates both by analyzing the resources they carry (i.e., human and social capital) and the situations they encounter (i.e., the type of city and extent of ethnic concentration in industries). Using this type of framework permits an examination of three competing explanations of the differences in attainment between some of the newest groups of foreign-born. *Members of certain immigrant groups may have different outcomes (1) because they are treated differently because of their race or ethnic origin; (2) because they possess varying levels of human and social capital; or (3) because they locate in cities where members of their ethnic group either create or find situations that are conducive to either success or failure.*

Since metropolitan areas most dramatically evidence the larger changes in ethnic stratification, five large U.S. cities serve as the focus of this research. New arrivals have revived the existing ethnic communities in many U.S. cities by re-infusing culture from their homelands and in the process have reinvigorated crumbling city social structures. Indeed, contemporary immigration is reshaping city landscapes by expanding previously existing ethnically heterogeneous labor markets and creating a strong ethnic entrepreneurial class. Ethnics are no longer limited to segregated ethnic economies because of widespread contact between ethnic and native-born workers and employers. Subsequently, many contemporary immigrants forge new paths to social and economic assimilation. On the other hand, those immigrants who arrive without skills or language proficiency may find themselves trapped in a new kind of urban barrio, a downgraded service economy devoid of institutional supports and stable work opportunities.

This study examines the immigrant experience in two types of cities, one globally connected with a heterogeneous foreign-born workforce (Immigrant Metropolis cities), and the other, a regionally centered city with a less ethnically heterogeneous workforce (Regional Centers). Three major cities, New York, Los Angeles, and Miami, serve as representative Immigrant Metropolis cities in this research. Each has a substantial foreign-born population, large industrial and service economies, and many international financial and commercial links. The other two urban centers, Atlanta and Denver, provide contrasts. These Regional Centers contain substantial minority populations, large regional economies, and are state capitals, but neither serves as a main immigrant destination.

Within these cities, this research centers on three Asian immigrant groups, Chinese, Filipino, and Korean, and two Latin American immigrant groups, Cuban and Mexican. These groups are representative of the latest immigrants to enter the U.S. By examining immigrants similar in racial and cultural backgrounds and different with respect to a series of structural variables, new insights can be gained

Table 1.3: Social and Economic Characteristics of Recent Immigrants by Year of Entry

	1980-90	Before 1990
Asian Indian		
% With college degree or higher[a]	52.6	65.3
% Does not speak English very well[b]	27.5	15.0
Median household income[c]	$35,587	$62,691
% Families below poverty line	11.5	3.6
African		
% With college degree or higher	44.1	50.5
% Does not speak English very well	28.2	16.5
Median household income	$27,762	$45,635
% Families below poverty line	18.8	6.6
Cambodian		
% With college degree or higher	4.3	12.0
% Does not speak English very well	73.9	58.1
Median household income	$16,435	$32,294
% Families below poverty line	46.6	19.7
Central American		
% With college degree or higher	7.3	9.1
% Does not speak English very well	74.4	60.7
Median household income	$20,197	$22,947
% Families below poverty line	25.6	16.2
Chinese		
% With college degree or higher	37.6	39.8
% Does not speak English very well	70.7	53.2
Median household income	$24,339	$44,641
% Families below poverty line	20.2	6.4
Cuban		
% With college degree or higher	7.4	17.3
% Does not speak English very well	73.3	56.0
Median household income	$21,622	$32,182
% Families below poverty line	23.2	8.6
Dominican		
% With college degree or higher	8.0	6.7
% Does not speak English very well	74.1	62.9
Median household income	$17,313	$19,333
% Families below poverty line	37.4	31.9

Table 1.3: Social and Economic Characteristics of Recent Immigrants by Year of Entry Continued

	1980-90	Before 1990
European		
% With college degree or higher	17.4	15.5
% Does not speak English very well	33.8	24.4
Median household income	$39,707	$40,524
% Families below poverty line	10.9	4.4
Filipino		
% With college degree or higher	44.9	40.4
% Does not speak English very well	38.2	26.5
Median household income	$40,693	$51,793
% Families below poverty line	6.7	3.6
Japanese		
% With college degree or higher	54.2	19.7
% Does not speak English very well	70.3	45.5
Median household income	$52,240	$43,010
% Families below poverty line	8.6	5.1
Korean		
% With college degree or higher	32.7	30.5
% Does not speak English very well	72.7	49.2
Median household income	$25,516	$44,358
% Families below poverty line	21.2	8.6
Mexican		
% With college degree or higher	4.4	3.0
% Does not speak English very well	78.1	63.3
Median household income	$17,429	$21,257
% Families below poverty line	34.8	24.1
Puerto Rican		
% With college degree or higher	9.8	9.7
% Does not speak English very well	53.9	45.3
Median household income	$18,859	$21,101
% Families below poverty line	34.0	23.9

Sources: 1990 Census of Population *CP-3-5, CP-3-3, CP-3-1.*
[a] Persons 25 years and older who have completed a Bachelor's Degree.
[b] Persons 25 years and older.
[c] 1989 dollars.

about current patterns of social and economic stratification. Furthermore, the relative successes of these five groups provide ample variation between and within groups in terms of the attainment indicators. Foreign-born non-Hispanic whites provide a standard for comparison.

An analysis that focuses on the human and social capital utilized by each group permits one to make inferences about the role of ethnic heritage in the attainment processes. Further, ecological context may jointly affect ethnic group stratification, so that Cubans in Miami, where dense ethnic networks and strong immigrant enterprises exist, may fare better in terms of income than Cubans in Denver, where they are one of the smallest immigrant groups living in the city. In comparison, Mexicans may fare better in Denver, where all sectors of the labor market are expanding, than in Los Angeles, where unskilled labor positions dominate. For example, do Mexicans fit the popular perception of the Latin American as migrant agricultural worker, whereas middle class Cuban immigrants do not? In fact, the Cuban immigration experience may have more in common with the Korean, while Chinese immigrants may have less in common with Filipino immigrants than with another non-Asian group. By examining the variation within Asian and Hispanic groups as well as between them, important distinctions can be assessed.

In sum, to answer the question of what accounts for ethnic differences in the experience of Asian and Hispanic immigrants in the U.S., this study examines ethnic heritage, human and social capital factors, and local labor market characteristics. This book examines these processes and looks at several ethnic groups from among two of the largest groups of contemporary immigrants to the U.S. Examination of the six immigrant groups in the selected metropolitan labor markets brings to light the influence of a changing industrial environment, skills and resources, and discrimination on social and economic attainment through a mix of history, theory, and descriptive and empirical analyses. Today's immigrants reflect much more diversity in terms of place of origin, race, and human capital than those who arrived at the dawn of the century. How well the groups are able to socially and economically assimilate into the U.S. will influence the future of racial and ethnic relations.

This research describes current immigration patterns and analyzes the resulting trends in ethnic stratification. Chapter 2 outlines the practical and ideological frameworks applied to immigration and reviews the relevant literature in the study of immigrant social and economic attainment. Chapter 3 describes the research design, data, and plan of analysis. The analysis and findings in Chapter 4 present the descriptive and empirical findings on current immigration patterns of five Asian and Latin American groups compared to foreign-born non-Hispanic whites. Chapter 5 concludes the study with a discussion of the significance and the implications of this research.

CHAPTER 2:
Practical, Ideological, and Theoretical Considerations

Crèvecoeur's (1782) inquiry, "What is an American?" captures the cultural dilemma of creating one unified identity out of the disparate immigrant groups who created the United States. Because immigrants did not represent a single coherent entity, the idea of a fusion of races, ethnic groups, and cultures to create a single American identity came to be reflected in the idea of the melting pot; the ideology used most often to describe U.S. ethnic relations.

Traditionally, social scientists have brought several interrelated interests to the study of immigration. Some focus on the *practical* issues and the policy concerns that immigration generates. One of the practical problems currently confronting immigration scholars is the absence of full assimilation for some groups of immigrants. Other scholars focus on understanding *ideological* issues, e.g., the public perceptions of immigrants, their experiences, and the process of immigrant social and economic attainment. Ideological questions arise over whether there is a dominant ideology applied to the immigrant experience and about what such an ideology might entail, e.g., assimilation, pluralism, or ethnic stratification. Finally, the goal of those who take a basic social scientific orientation to the study of immigration is the description and explanation of immigrant social and economic attainment. The central *theoretical* question asks what factors lead to assimilation and or away from it, and more generally, how the processes that involve those factors work (Cohen 1989). The theoretical framework scientifically explains ethnic differences in social and economic attainment.

15

Historically, the study of immigration has been central to the discipline of sociology.[2] Sociology is concerned with understanding integrative processes and social integration, the process through which disparate social units fit together to form a smoothly working whole (Parsons 1951). By studying immigrants, social scientists have learned not only about general patterns of assimilation, but also about the institutions that foster or impede its processes. Today the study of immigration remains central to the field of sociology. Studies that focus on how immigrant groups adapt to a new society reveal whether group characteristics and the resources they possess enhance or impede assimilation. They also consider how the opportunity structure of the host society influences ethnic stratification. Current differences in the economic standing of U.S. immigrant groups suggest that they may take different pathways to complete social and economic assimilation. Some of these groups manage quite well and often exceed the median household earnings for native-born white Americans. Others continue to fall below the poverty line. The implications of multiple modes of immigrant attainment could change some of the popular perceptions held about immigrants, e.g., as leveling down the quality of life. Additionally, understanding why some immigrant groups do not fare well economically may provide insight into the persistent racial and ethnic inequality present in the contemporary U.S.

The central question this research explores is what accounts for ethnic variation in social and economic attainment among contemporary immigrants. Contemporary immigrants have a range of experiences and varying degrees of adaptation to the U.S. Full assimilation implies that immigrant and native-born groups have similar levels of economic well-being, e.g., comparable mean household incomes, similar distributions of educational attainment, attitudes, beliefs, values, etc. Social and economic stratification may still exist, however *ethnic* stratification would not. Patterns of assimilation depend on the characteristics of the entering groups, including race or cultural markers, as well as the features of the host society, for example, the characteristics of local labor markets and ethnic communities.

---

[2] For example, see some of the classic sociological studies of immigrant communities: Thomas and Znaniecki, *The Polish Peasant*; Gans, *Urban Villagers*; Handlin, *The Uprooted*; Whyte, *Street Corner Society*.

The recent literature suggests that there are several modes of social and economic attainment. Immigrants tend to concentrate in different kinds of occupations. Some immigrant groups provide disproportionately more professionals and managers, while others are more entrepreneurial. Other groups rely on manual labor or service sector jobs. The outcomes of their experiences vary: some groups integrate economically and socially, while others show little adaptation. The substantial variation in immigrant attainment may be due in part to the variation in the extent to which immigrants share cultural, social, and economic similarities with native-born groups. Foreign-born non-Hispanic whites serve as an appropriate standard of comparison for the five ethnic groups in this sample because this group most closely resembles the mainstream white population. Many of the native-born whites are of the same ethnic origin as these recent immigrants, which means that their social and economic attainment may follow a generally less difficult path.

PRACTICAL ISSUES

With 19.8 million foreign-born counted in the 1990 Census along with the estimated one million who have arrived each year since, immigrants are currently responsible for the largest component of population growth in the U.S. Their social and economic well-being unquestionably is central to the health of the U.S. as a whole. However, their ultimate effect on political, economic, and social structures is yet unknown.

The newest immigrants are heterogeneous along several dimensions: racial/ethnic background, sex ratios, education and work experience, and ties to old and new receiving communities. Given their inter-group diversity, their abilities to adapt to the U.S. raise interesting questions concerning whether ethnicity, individual skill sets, or contextual factors such as local labor market conditions create different destinies for them. It is not clear whether variation on contextual factors impedes or enhances their social and economic attainment as a whole.

Today's immigrants are different from those who arrived in the past, and the situations in which they find themselves are different as well. Accordingly, the ability of the nation to absorb these groups requires a closer look at their experiences. The evidence of increasing stratification within and between foreign-born groups, and also as compared to native-born groups, indicates that how well these groups ultimately fare is important to the future of U.S. racial and ethnic relations. When some groups remain segregated at the bottom of the economic queue while others move ahead, a host of problems, including inter-ethnic conflict are created. The full societal impact of large groups that are unable to fully participate in the economic and social arenas is not clear.

Other practical issues arise as a consequence of immigration. The question of how immigrants affect social and economic institutions has re-ignited national debate over the future of immigration policy. Policy analysts and public interest groups are split over whether immigrants are responsible for taking jobs away from native-born workers, or whether their labor fuels economic growth. Because many of the new immigrants come from the Third World, the perception of this wave as unskilled and uneducated is pervasive. Because of that perception, many claim that the quality of life in the U.S. is declining. Immigrants have been blamed for an increase in crime, drains on health care and other social services, and the declining quality of public education. The increase in illegal immigration adds credence to the idea that the U.S. has lost control of its national borders and is becoming, in Peter Brimelow's (1995) words, an "alien nation."

Without a doubt, the change in predominant origin of immigrants has altered the fundamental racial and ethnic composition of the U.S. Immigrants of the past are thought of as similar to those groups who emerged from the melting pot as "Americans," whereas today's non-white immigrants are characterized as unmeltable or unassimilatable. Many fear that immigrants today do not want to become Americans; they point to government programs that encourage immigrants to retain their distinctive ethnic and racial identities and languages, e.g., multi-lingual ballots and multi-lingual citizenship exams. Should this "cult of ethnicity" be permitted to continue, some fear the U.S. will risk losing its bonds of cohesion and become Balkanized (Schlesinger 1992). Others, like Richard Lamm and Gary Imhoff (1985: 97-8) write that unassimilated immigrants have the power to change the U.S. into a "splintered nation, divided by separate languages, separate cultures, separate traditions" and their impact will result in a "radical overturning of our way of life...[creating a] clash and conflict of differing cultures within our country."

The shift in immigration from primarily European origins to Latin American and Asian origins also raises public concerns about the future of ethnic stratification in the U.S. Historically, Hispanic Americans have stood at the bottom of the stratification system along with African Americans and American Indians. Some fear that if Hispanic immigration flows continue, then large numbers of Hispanic Americans may overburden the U.S. social support system. Asian immigrants raise other concerns. Even though they are typically viewed by the pubic as "model minorities," some of the newer Asian immigrants are not able to adapt rapidly, while others seem disinterested in fully adopting American culture. This perceived threat of a large number of unassimilatable non-white immigrants continues to reverberate in media characterizations of new immigration as the "browning of America."

IDEOLOGICAL CONCERNS

With immigration raising many practical concerns among native-born Americans, the common understanding of a single American identity shapes many individual responses to immigration and immigrants themselves. The ideological frames of immigration and the pathways to success in this country reveal the state of ethnic and racial relations among different segments of the population. The way the American people view the immigrant adaptation process creates assumptions about why particular groups advance while others do not. Individuals formulate attitudes and expectations about immigrants based in part on the particular immigrant adaptation ideology.

In the U.S., we commonly use the ideologies of multiculturalism, the melting pot, assimilation, cultural pluralism, and continued ethnic stratification to describe the consequences of immigration and contact with groups who differ from the mainstream in some manner (Gordon 1961). Each ideology conveys a different response to Crèvecoeur's question of what it takes to become an American. Whether any particular metaphor or ideology closely mirrors the actual experiences of immigrants is not clear. Studying ideology provides a glimpse into the national character and the state of relations among segments of the population.

In an attempt to understand the establishment and maintenance of community, social, and political order in the U.S., early immigration theorists were influenced by the national ideology of the melting pot. From a practical standpoint, this ideology reveals public assumptions more than theoretical analysis. Yet, the melting pot, or more generally assimilation,[3] remains the most persistent metaphor of the immigrant experience in the U.S.

A recurrent theme in U.S. history is that the American experience produces a new kind of individual, forged from the immigrant stock of risk-takers seeking a new life. By leaving behind their traditions, cultures, and prejudices, and by making a new life under harsh conditions, early immigrants to America created a new and stronger society. The melting pot metaphor asserts that the unique conditions in the U.S. mix and reshape immigrants to produce a superior "race" of people. In their adaptation to society, immigrants contribute something new to the existing culture even as they adapt to it.

One of the early proponents of the melting pot, Crèvecoeur (1782 [1912]), identified what he called a "new race" of Americans who were indeed different from their foreign-born ancestors, not so much by blood, but by experience. Their new life required shifts in manners, thoughts, and identity (Crèvecoeur 1782 [1912]). Over a century later, Frederick Jackson Turner's *Frontier Thesis* firmly echoed this sentiment. For Turner, life on the frontier was the dominant influence on American institutions and the origin of an American character. It was responsible for the creation of a "composite nationality" so that its inhabitants were "English in neither nationality nor characteristics" (Turner 1920 [1983]: 22-23). The challenge of life on the frontier created the conditions that made cooperation between individuals essential. The danger of attacks by American Indians, the unpredictable weather, and the distance from civilized life along the eastern seaboard necessitated mutual dependence and the abandonment of old world prejudices among the inhabitants on the frontier. This theme was echoed elsewhere because of the frontier's influence on American life.

---

[3] Assimilation is a term that actually describes two forms of adaptation: incorporation (Anglo conformity) and amalgamation (melting pot). The principal motive for many who take an ideological stance that promotes assimilation is their desire to maintain American institutions. Thus, while the melting pot metaphor is held as the standard they support, their rhetoric is more consistent with the incorporative form of assimilation.

The literature of that era further reflects the romantic notion of the American melting pot as spoken by the character of David, the young Russian-Jewish musician in Israel Zangwill's 1909 play aptly titled, *The Melting Pot:*

> There she lies, the great Melting Pot -- listen! Can't you hear the roaring and the bubbling? There gapes her mouth – the harbor where a thousand mammoth feeders come from the ends of the world to pour in their human freight. Ah, what a stirring and a seething! Celt and Latin, Slav and Teuton, Greek and Syrian -- black and yellow. ... East and West, and North and South, the palm and the pine, the pole and the equator, the crescent and the cross -- How the great Alchemist melts and fuses them with his purging flame! Here shall they all unite to build the Republic of Man and the Kingdom of God. Ah, Vera, what is the glory of Rome and Jerusalem, where all races and nations come to worship and look back, compared with the glory of America, where all races and nations come to labor and look forward! (Pp. 184-185).

The idea of a fusion of races that creates a superior breed of American is neither new to our history, nor will it fade away in the near future. It has come to define the true American spirit of individuality and a chance for success. If immigrants can adapt to American life, they can make it as successful Americans.

This ideological model claims that once immigrants adapt to the American system, they can succeed. That is, the melting pot takes them as outsiders and converts them into Americans. With persistence and hard work, they are then able to succeed as all Americans do. However, when members of ethnic groups continue to differ from the mainstream after they have taken on "American" characteristics, the American dream is undermined. These implicit assumptions about how adaptation occurs frame the way different ethnic groups are treated. If the assumptions about what defines Americans include a clear vision of how to become one, then those who diverge from that path are held outside the system. There is no room for understanding persistent inequality or ethnic conflict from the melting pot perspective.

Although assimilation may be a goal of both immigrant and native-born ethnic groups, it may also be possible that some members of both groups may view it as undesirable. Assimilation, as a belief, a goal, or a structural pattern, does help explain some inter-group relations. The framework is appealing because it suggests that all groups can succeed in society through self-reliance and hard work. However, it understates the existence of structural barriers and discrimination that might impede mobility. Many contemporary Americans hold onto their belief in this ideology— consider the support for legislation that guarantees English as the national language and the opposition to bilingual education.

Despite the persistence of these ideas, assimilation and the melting pot do not mesh with the experiences of many contemporary immigrants. A uniform process of assimilation is an implausible precondition for immigrant social and economic success. Socio-economic attainment in the U.S. is a complex process that depends only partially on the motivation and abilities immigrants bring to the social and economic marketplace with them. How they are able to use those resources often depends upon the prior history of the group to which they belong and how they are received by native-born groups.

THEORETICAL PERSPECTIVES

Accounting for differences in the immigrant experience is the most important task of scientific sociology. Theories of ethnic stratification explain why some immigrant groups succeed while others do not. With a sound theoretical framework, social scientists can provide insight into the differences in the social and economic attainment of the U.S. foreign-born. This can then serve as the basis for more informed policy decisions and more accurate public perceptions of the social and economic successes (and failures) of certain ethnic groups. Explaining ethnic stratification among immigrant groups may further the understanding of ethnic stratification among native-born ethnic groups as well.

The social sciences offer a variety of explanations for differences in the social and economic attainment of recent immigrants to the U.S. The focus in this research rests primarily on the sociological and social psychological theories[4] developed to account for that variation. In general, there are two varieties of approaches, those that address the individual or group factors and others that address ecological or community level factors. The first claims that the character of attributes of the groups (skills and abilities) explains social and economic attainment. The second asserts that the explanation lies in the features of the host society. This section begins with a brief review of each perspective, then suggests the importance of a synthesis of the two perspectives.

The Race Relations Cycle

The historic and most influential understanding of immigration comes from Park and Burgess' (1921) contact hypothesis. This argument posits that an evolutionary cycle of contact, competition, accommodation, and assimilation characterizes the experiences of immigrants in a host society. The race relations cycle resounds closely with the ideology of the melting pot, since the ultimate outcome of amalgamation eliminates ethnic boundaries and restores equilibrium to a system stressed by inter-group conflict. The race relations cycle describes several intermediate outcomes that result from sustained ethnic contact including the development of ethnic hierarchies.[5] The successive stages of competition and conflict are inevitable in the cycle because sustained contact between different cultures is likely to induce disputes over resources (Brown 1934). From this perspective, conflict is a struggle for position in the economic order. Accommodation is possible only after inter-group differences are resolved through competition and conflict (Park and Burgess 1921). The next stage, assimilation, is the final step in social integration. It involves a more complete transformation in which individuals share tradition and

---

[4] In addition to the social psychological perspective on ethnic variation in economic stratification, there are a series of (well-disputed) biological and genetic arguments to explain ethnic differences. Because this work rests on the understanding of race and ethnicity as social constructs, biological explanations are not discussed.

[5] Noel (1968) claims that ethnocentrism and relative power differences are necessary elements of ethnic stratification.

experience to forge a common cultural life—similar character, thought, and institutions created from culturally divergent beginnings.

According to Park and Burgess (1921), assimilation is primarily a psychological fusion rather than a biological transformation, closely akin to the growing alike of character and personality. Whereas other accommodations are temporary re-organizations of social relations to reduce and manage ethnic conflict, full assimilation restores social equilibrium by eradicating distinct boundaries between ethnic groups and precluding competition from reappearing. Within this context, assimilation merely represents a stable societal outcome of inter-group contact— an absence of ethnic distinctions and the boundaries associated with them.

Inter-group boundaries slowly erode throughout the race relations cycle, starting with ecological, political, and economic boundaries, and ending at the personal and cultural levels (Park 1950). With attempts to maintain social order at each level, race relations are themselves inherently unstable, since they invariably assume contact and conflict. The race relations cycle can terminate only once a stable inter-group configuration is achieved, one in which ethnic competition is precluded. In the absence of strict laws that maintain social distance, assimilation is inevitable, because it restores social equilibrium through the eradication of ethnic boundaries:

> [Assimilation is] progressive and irreversible. Customs regulations, immigration restrictions and racial barriers may slacken the tempo of the movement; may perhaps halt it altogether for a time; but cannot change its direction; cannot at any rate, reverse it (Park 1950: 150).

In this framework, stable, or non-competitive ethnic relations in some instances can be achieved temporarily by group subordination, although other outcomes can reduce the significance of ethnic boundaries. The boundaries created between the different levels of the hierarchy should either re-establish order and equilibrium in the system, or decrease the degree of niche overlap and ethnic contact. Only assimilation and exclusion permanently prevent ethnic conflict from re-emerging. Because assimilation is a form of social, cultural, and racial fusion in which at least one cultural identity is incorporated into a larger one, ethnic distinctions disappear entirely. On the other hand, exclusion can take several forms, caste or legal systems that formally distance the minority group from the majority group and physical or geographic separation of the minority group through relocation or genocide. In contrast to assimilation and exclusion, cultural pluralism and symbiosis do not imply group subordination. E. Barth and Noel (1972) detail these forms of accommodation that reduce niche overlap and promote stable ethnic boundaries in the short run. In symbiosis, members of distinct ethnic groups develop an exchange system. They are able to voluntarily maintain a degree of separateness without stratification because of mutual dependence. Pluralism is another form of accommodation that reduces ethnic conflict. It describes a system of inter-group relations in which ethnic distinctions continue to exist without group subordination. In heterogeneous societies such as the U.S., some ethnic minorities maintain their cultural traditions, yet carry on essentially egalitarian relationships with members of the larger society. They participate in many American social and economic institutions, speak English, and become citizens. The last outcome of inter-ethnic conflict, continued ethnic stratification, implies that interaction between unequal groups maintains minority group subordination. The groups remain segregated economically and politically, by either a legal or a social system that sets the two apart as separate and unequal. Although cultural pluralism, egalitarian symbiosis, and continued stratification may reduce ethnic conflict and promote stability for an indefinite period of time, these ethnic configurations may eventually disintegrate and begin the cycle of competition and conflict anew because ethnic differences and boundaries remain.

Although the race relations cycle suggests that the stages in the process of adaptation lead to a reduction of stratification, it does not explain why ethnic groups may hold different positions in this system of stratification. An additional difficulty with the race relations cycle is that it does not specify the amount of time spent in each stage, nor does it outline how the transition from stage to stage occurs. Inter-group variation in terms of the level of competition or conflict experienced is also not clear. Some groups experience relatively little conflict as they move through the race relations cycle, while other groups face extreme exclusionary measures to curtail potential economic competition. It is also difficult to falsify the theory since it has no time constraints. Future assimilation has the potential to occur at some unspecified time for all groups who have not experienced it. The actual patterns of ethnic differences in the U.S. are not consistent with the race relations cycle. Accommodation is inhibited in some groups, and many ethnic groups have not yet reached the final stage of assimilation. These observations suggest that other arguments may explain the processes that govern immigrant attainment. The evidence of increasing ethnic stratification and the search for better explanations are the motivations of the following theory review. In the remainder of this chapter, I discuss alternative explanations for ethnic stratification among immigrants.

Economics of Discrimination

Discrimination is one mechanism that is used to explain ethnic differences in income, earnings, and other social and economic outcomes. This perspective implies that variation in economic attainment can be accounted for by discrimination based on race/ethnic prejudices and faulty or inflexible characterizations of ethnic background by employers, employees, or consumers. Data examining racial and ethnic prejudice reveal a transformation of white racial attitudes towards blacks and other minorities with respect to housing, education, and occupational issues since the early 1970s (Schuman and Steeh 1996; Schuman and Bobo 1988). Yet, given this apparent decline in race prejudice,[6] the number of discriminatory actions that stem from perceived racial differences is alarming, as are the disparities in median family income, educational attainment and residential segregation that remain.

The economics of discrimination argument describes how ethnic background and differences in earnings are connected. In essence, the argument asserts that if individuals have a distaste for outgroups, then they must be compensated for associating with members of those

---

[6] There are several types of prejudices: cognitive, affective, and conative. Cognitive prejudices imply that members of different groups have different skills or abilities which forms the basis of prejudice, while affective prejudices attach valences or evaluations to the attributes one associates with the groups compared. Conative prejudices, on the other hand, are attitudes that express a propensity to act based on the cognitive or affective prejudices.

ethnic groups (Becker 1957). For example, when the members of the majority group are conatively prejudiced and are negatively predisposed toward working with members of an immigrant minority, they incur a cost if contact is not restricted in some manner. When this occurs, workers calculate the strength of their prejudice against their desire for income and choose the option that best maximizes either their economic or emotional return to investments. That is, if whites incur an emotional cost for working around minorities, they will seek a higher wage to overcome this cost. From an employer's perspective, for example, it would cost more to employ white workers alongside black workers than it would to maintain a homogenous work force. Alternatively, employers can recoup the higher labor cost by paying minority workers a lower wage.

Employers compare the intensity of their own conative prejudices with the costs of that prejudice and determine the action that brings the maximum net return. Native-born employers also incur psychological costs when they employ immigrants. They could compensate for this cost by increasing their prices, but this would put them at a competitive disadvantage. In turn, they could extract the cost from the immigrants that they hire. Immigrants thus would be paid less than native-born workers. In this way, native-born employers could make up the cost of interacting with immigrants by paying them less, and native-born workers would be "compensated" for working with immigrants by being paid more. Thus, discrimination occurs when pay or income is forfeited and considerations of productivity are ignored in determining hiring practices in order to deny jobs or income to certain classes of workers.

Some forms of discrimination may be positively related to the overall number of ethnics employed in a certain market. As the numerical importance of a group grows (or the perception of its growth grows), so does the potential to trigger discrimination from the majority group (Becker 1957). Discrimination in this way is the outcome of competition, either real or perceived, between ethnics and non-ethnics for wages, jobs, or power. That is, if native-born workers perceive that immigrants undercut their wages, then as immigration grows, certain groups may be targeted for discrimination. This may explain why in an era of increasing numbers of Asians and Latinos looking for work in the U.S., wage discrepancies persist between those groups and native-born workers. Status differences partly determine levels of discrimination and prejudice as well. When two groups of unequal status come into contact, the greater the status gap between them, the more likely it is for prejudice to increase (Allport 1955). The economics of discrimination argument implies that some groups should receive higher incomes and better jobs solely as consequence of their racial or ethnic status because of employer prejudice. Groups more similar to the dominant groups should therefore receive better positions and pay. Furthermore, groups for whom there is greater tolerance should get more valued outcomes than those for whom there is less tolerance. I summarize the argument in Hypothesis 1.

H1.   Ethnic/race attainment outcomes vary inversely with discrimination. The more ethnic discrimination that exists, the lower the social and economic attainments of immigrants (Economics of Discrimination).

Human and Social Capital

The economics of discrimination perspective underscores employer discrimination based on characteristics not directly correlated with labor market productivity i.e., ethnic background. However, it is economically irrational to hire whites in a system if they require a higher wage than minority workers. Similar to the economics of discrimination, human capital theory explains income discrepancy in terms of discrimination. However, human capital theory posits that discrimination occurs based on characteristics associated with labor market productivity, i.e., skills, training, and education (Becker 1993 [1964]). Therefore, human capital theory describes economically rational discrimination. One rationally chooses those workers whose skills portend the best work for the lowest cost.

Human capital refers to abilities such as education, training, and skills that are presumed to have value in the marketplace. The theory claims that because employers pay more to those who make greater investments in themselves, employee job prestige increases, and other workplace rewards add to the benefits of the human capital investments (Becker 1993 [1964]; Mincer 1974, 1993). In fact, much of the social inequality in income can be traced to variation in education and training (Becker 1993 [1964]). The importance of education is well documented in increasing earnings and productivity, as more highly educated and skilled individuals tend to earn more than others do. This argument extends to immigrants as well. Highly skilled and educated immigrants are better able to adjust to new positions in the U.S. than unskilled and less educated immigrants. For immigrants, higher educational qualifications and facility with English lessen the reliance on the informal ethnic economy for gainful employment. Immigrants who lack skill in English or local labor market experience look to ethnic firms for jobs and rely heavily on personal networks to find jobs (Chiswick 1978).

The focus on individual resources emphasizes achievement based on accumulated investments in skills and abilities. Human capital theory implies that whether an individual possesses the right values, ethic, education, and skills significantly affects where she or he will be placed in the occupational hierarchy. Employers discriminate against potential workers who do not have the characteristics that presumably correlate with productivity, for example, language facility, knowledge of local business practices, and credentials and references that translate into success in the U.S.

Other theorists extend the idea of human capital to include other forms of capital. Bourdieu (1986) elaborates on three forms of capital: economic; cultural, i.e., educational credentials or certain dispositions; and social, i.e., titles of nobility or social connections. The ways in which individuals and families use cultural and social capital are their strategies of status distinctions (Bourdieu 1986). The cultural and social forms of capital emphasize competence in practices that can ultimately be converted into financial capital, for example educational credentials or social connections. Building on Bourdieu (1983) and Coleman (1988), Portes and Sensenbrenner (1993) argue that social capital functions as a material resource in the same manner as human capital does, because it links the individual to the larger social structure of the community. Investments in social capital are defined as "expectations for action within a collectivity that affect the economic goals and goal seeking behavior of its members, even if those expectations are not oriented toward the economic sphere" (Portes and Sensenbrenner 1993: 1323). These expectations of action bind the individual to the ethnic community and serve to increase his/her economic prospects.

Social capital can also limit the goal-seeking behavior of a group. It may prohibit the individual from maximizing her/his interests at the expense of other members of the ethnic community. This reformulation of collective expectations as an ethnic resource resounds with Young's (1993) connection between solidarity and the problem solving capacity of a community. In this way, collective identity may serve to strengthen the trust imbued in ethnic networks and aid in the attainment process overall. Information about housing and available jobs as well as assisting in finding childcare or transportation often stems from the connections fostered by social capital.

According to Sanders and Nee (1996), immigrant families manifest social and cultural investments made prior to immigration. Family-based strategies are a mechanism for mobility that draw on a mix of social, cultural, and economic capital. Family members rely upon this capital throughout the assimilation process, as these social resources help to ease the strain of relocating to a new area and establishing a new way of life. Family and friendship networks provide information and access to community resources as well (Sanders and Nee 1996). Especially when beginning self-employment, immigrants often use the capital embodied in their household to offset deficiencies in their individual human or economic capital (Sanders and Nee 1996). "Hiring" family members and pooling economic resources situates the household as the main source of capital, rather than the individual. The goal of this mobility strategy is a collective good rather than individual gain, as the family acts as a repository of support within the binding ethnic network of the larger community. Immigrants who do not possess substantial financial capital may rely solely on the social and cultural capital investments of their family to ease their integration into the new society.

In examining obstacles to immigrant social and economic attainment, discrimination arguments seek to explain ethnic stratification in terms of ethnic characteristics or of ethnic differences on traits that are presumed to directly affect productivity. This perspective adds to the understanding of why certain ethnic groups are able to assimilate rapidly, while others do so at a slower pace, and still others cannot make economic progress. Examining capital investments of individuals and families leads to an additional understanding of modes of attainment. I summarize arguments based on theories of human and social capital in Hypothesis 2.

H2. Ethnic/race differences in social and economic attainments vary directly with investment in human and social capital. The greater the investments, the higher the social and economic attainment (Human and Social Capital Theories).

Competition Theories

Under the broad framework of competition theory, many conceptual models describe immigrant adaptation and the position of immigrant groups in the labor market with respect to boundary overlap and niche. Instead of assuming the placement of immigrant groups into arbitrarily ordered production slots, competition theory assumes that placement in the occupational hierarchy is based on competitive advantages and disadvantages. Competition theories describe the role the host society plays as a receiving context characterized by uncertainty and stress for some immigrants.

Competition theories contend that an absolute threat of resource competition may not be the only spark to conflict. A perceived threat can ignite ethnic antagonism as well (Olzak 1992). In other words, evidence of direct competition for resources may initiate inter-group conflict, however the simple threat of direct competition, real or imagined, can also ignite ethnic antagonism.

Many theorists agree that the creation of ethnic divisions within a population is intricately enmeshed with the mechanisms that foster class divisions. Accordingly, the failure of ethnicity to erode in significance stems from reasons other than its cultural persistence, reasons that instead are linked to class position (Blauner 1972). In examining what she terms "successful" minorities, Bonacich (1973) suggests that some immigrants come to occupy an economic niche between producers and consumers, one that other ethnic groups refuse or are barred from filling.[7] Despite prejudice and hostility, these anomalous groups gain economic mobility by filling this economic niche and reaping the benefits. However, their intermediary merchant role coupled with economic success often attracts a high degree of hostility from the host society (Bonacich 1973). To compensate for this, these groups exhibit

---

[7]See Loewen (1988) and Quan (1982) for detailed ethnographic work on Chinese grocers in the Mississippi delta region who fill the economic niche between white producers and black consumers.

high levels of internal solidarity, which may further limit their social and economic attainment. Ironically their middleman niche facilitates their economic success and simultaneously delays their social integration. Yet, the middleman niche permits some groups substantial advantages compared to other less well-situated groups.

The role of ethnic solidarity in the adaptation process is not well understood, given that the strength of an ethnic boundary may either facilitate economic mobility or perpetuate ethnic segregation. It may maintain group cohesiveness and pride on the one hand, or increase economic antagonism and conflict. In fact, ecological and competition theorists argue that ethnic solidarity increases with inter-group competition over resources (F. Barth 1969; Hannan 1979; Ragin 1979; Olzak 1983). In contrast to the race relations cycle, some competition theorists do not view competition as a distinct evolutionary process on the road to complete assimilation, but rather as the beginning of a cycle of boundary overlap,[8] conflict, exclusion, and sustained inequality.

Bonacich (1972) argues that ethnic group position in a labor market is a function of variations in human and social capital. Differences in economic, informational, and political resources set the price of wages. Individuals with fewer resources receive lower wages. Ethnic differences eventually become indicators of this capital. Bonacich contends that human and social capital differences are superceded by conative prejudices. In a split labor market,[9] competition over resources increases both group solidarity and ethnic conflict. Employers seek to maximize profit and maintain a docile labor force by employing the lowest wage group, in this case, immigrants and minorities who have fewer resources than the native-born group. This action places the lower wage and the higher wage groups in competition for limited positions. In this way, employers use immigrants to undercut the wages of native workers. According to

---

[8] Boundary or niche overlap occurs when two or more groups compete for the same social and economic resources (e.g., housing, jobs, and education). The ensuing conflict will end once stable ethnic relations are imposed through institutionalized segregation or exclusion (Barth 1969; Olzak 1983).

[9] A labor market is defined as "split" if there are "at least two groups of workers whose price differs for the same work, or would differ if they did the same work" (Bonacich 1972: 549).

Bonacich (1972), the progression out of the stage of competition and conflict occurs when the more powerful group either institutes exclusionary measures to keep the less powerful group out of the labor market, or institutes a caste system or social hierarchy that serves a similar purpose. Either of these outcomes establishes equilibrium as defined by competition theorists since the degree of niche overlap is reduced and inter-group competition is eliminated.

Differences in power and resources lead to conditions that ultimately advantage majority labor. In the U.S. for example, if whites are a substantial majority in the laboring class, they can coerce labor policy in their favor. In this case, exclusionary immigration policy could sustain the under-supply of labor and the advantaged position of white labor as it did in the 1920s. Here Bonacich reconciles the seemingly irrational act of hiring white workers at higher wages rather than immigrant or minority workers at lower wages. Employers in this scenario are influenced by the political power of the majority labor.

Well-defined and rigidly enforced ethnic boundaries often create hostility between native groups and new workers. Perceiving immigrants as an economic threat, native workers have, in the past, attempted to maintain ethnic boundaries by practicing exclusionist tactics: e.g., barring minorities from unions, lobbying for immigration quotas, or intimidating minorities and immigrants through physical violence. As the antagonism from outside groups increases, so does the minority group's internal solidarity. Within these minority groups, individuals recognize their similar economic position and identify with each other based on their ethnic distinctiveness, consequently reinforcing their sense of ethnic commonalities (Hechter 1978; Cummings 1972). Although ethnic solidarity and labor market participation are intrinsically linked, this connection has not always been addressed in the immigrant adaptation literature. Most studies of economic attainment focus on what makes jobs appealing (i.e., labor market rewards or segmentation) or what makes people good workers (i.e., skill, training, and education). Several theories, however, can be tied together to analyze both positions.

Dual and Segmented Labor Markets

One of the frameworks that examines the structural economic sector, the "demand side" perspective, has profoundly influenced immigrant adaptation theories. Traditionally, dual labor market theories dominated economic research aimed at explaining the placement of immigrants into the occupational hierarchy. According to this framework, labor markets in free societies are divided into two distinct economic sectors: the core, the large scale industries that monopolize power and resources; and the periphery, the small scale companies in marginal lines of production (Gordon, Edwards, and Reich 1988).

Segmented labor market theories extend the characteristics of the competitive economic environment to the organization of the labor markets within each sector. As such, primary labor markets exist mainly in the core sector, while secondary labor markets are more likely to be found in the peripheral sector (Piore 1975). Jobs in the core sector and primary labor market receive more benefits than those in the periphery— the jobs are stable, wages are high, and internal job ladders are present (Reich, Gordon, and Edwards 1973). Due to lack of skills or local labor market experience, newly arrived immigrants find jobs mainly in the secondary labor market (Chiswick 1982). Given that the boundary between the primary and secondary labor markets is not easily permeable, it follows that the social and economic assimilation of some groups, especially culturally distinct immigrant groups, is difficult because their individual characteristics combine with market characteristics to differentially place them in secondary markets. Immigrants have fewer skills and less local labor market experience and thus are more likely to fall into the poorly paid, low-status sectors. In sum, these heuristic schemes are dichotomizations of the labor market based on technological and worker characteristics. These arguments are summarized in Hypothesis 3.

H3. Differences in workers' social and economic attainments vary with their positions in dual or segmented labor markets (Dual Labor Market Theories).

Other researchers have maintained that in addition to the primary and secondary economies, a third sector exists to ease the costs to immigration, the enclave economy (Wilson and Portes 1980). An ethnic enclave consists of a residential and commercial concentration of ethnic workers bound together by personal networks. Because the majority of immigrants relocate to areas that have a large percentage of residents from their country of origin, the enclave is continually renewed. The enclave is protected from the open labor market and serves as a culturally and linguistically familiar niche in which past investments in human capital may be recognized and rewarded. Foreign credentials are valued here, which gives immigrants more bargaining power than if they were to work in the primary or secondary economies (Wilson and Bach 1985). These ethnic communities create social and economic support for the newcomers and make their transition into a new culture more fluid. By operating outside the economic mainstream, ethnic economies encounter less regulation and interference from local government, allow employers and workers greater job flexibility, and create conditions for mobility inside the community. Portes and Bach (1985: 203) describe an ethnic enclave as:

> (1) the presence of immigrants with sufficient capital, either brought from abroad or accumulated in the U.S. to create new opportunities for economic growth, and (2) an extensive division of labor. Typically, this division develops through the transplantation of an entrepreneurial class from origin to destination during the first waves of migration.

However, whether the enclave functions positively for all inhabitants or only for those who own a small business remains a question (Sanders and Nee 1987; Zhou and Logan 1991). Within the enclave, the personal connections of kinship and ethnic solidarity are intense and may lead employers to exploit their co-ethnic workers as cheap sources of labor (Becker 1957; Evans 1989). For example, family members are not always paid for their labor, which allows more money to be reinvested into the business (Quan 1982). Sanders and Nee (1987) focus on the differential opportunities that exist within the confines of the enclave. They recognize it as a divided labor market that creates different opportunities and working conditions for workers and bosses.

Although the ensuing research on the enclave economy hypothesis has spurred scholarly interest, there has been little systematic understanding of where the exact boundaries of the enclave economy lie (Nee et al 1994; Waldinger 1993; Bonacich and Modell 1988). Problems exist in the conceptualization of the enclave, whether defined by industrial sector, spatial concentration, place of residence, or place of work. Furthermore, the lack of fine-grained data through which this dilemma could be resolved poses a barrier. The debate over the contours of the enclave has introduced some amount of skepticism as to the beneficial effects of working in an ethnically segregated community. Despite the heuristic appeal of these ideas of a sharply divided economy and of ethnically stratified labor markets, little empirical evidence supports their distinct existence (Wallace and Kalleberg 1982; Baron and Bielby 1984; Ryan 1981). However, evidence concerning points at the extremes exists. Large powerful companies with formal job ladders, such as Microsoft or AT&T, contrast with small family owned businesses with no room for employee career development, such as local restaurants or small retail stores. Nonetheless, the failure to find a distinct demarcation between the two industrial sectors of the ethnic economy does not indicate the absence of all segmentation (Ryan 1981). However, the intermediate area between the extremes is much more difficult to characterize.

The most recent perspective on this problem has been to accept the existence of ethnic economy and to forgo the task of determining the exact position of the enclave's frontier. Nee et al (1994) contend that a continuous distribution of firms, size, market power, and ethnic content may more aptly describe the U.S. economy. Ethnic economies are integrated with the larger urban environment, somewhat like ethnic niches dispersed throughout urban economies that incorporate a multi-ethnic labor force and clientele (Nee et al 1994). Ethnic economies are thus similar to open economies as there is variation in the degree of ethnic content. For example, non-ethnic workers and ethnic workers may be employed by ethnic bosses to serve multi-ethnic customers. There is no dichotomous ethnic/non-ethnic break in the economy. However, the conceptual term is quite useful in describing the different environments within which some ethnics live and work.   Ethnic businesses and workers are more concentrated in these environments, but are just not concisely defined.

Two axes structure ethnic economies: the density of ethnic ties and the degree of firm formality (Nee et al 1994). They range from very low ethnic density among groups that are fully integrated into the mainstream economy to very high ethnic density among members of groups that are relegated to closed ethnic economies. Additionally, firm formality ranges from informal work arrangements to formal institutionalized operations at the workplace. Most businesses operate somewhere along the middle of this grid, combining characteristics of ethnic and non-ethnic resources and formal and informal practices. Both workers and employers maneuver their way through the entire mixed economy. In addition to labor market sector, self-employment or ethnic entrepreneurship often plays an important role in immigrant social and economic attainment. The fact that much of the contemporary analysis of immigration focuses on ethnic enterprise is not surprising given the reliance on the growth of the ethnic firm as a means toward mobility (Light and Bonacich 1988; Bonacich 1995). Ethnic economies have transformed many center cities by supporting a large immigrant workforce and many ethnic businesses. Unable to find jobs that provide substantial returns to prior human capital investments, many immigrants start small businesses. These businesses can benefit from a captive market for culturally defined products and informal sources of credit (Portes and Zhou 1992). Family members provide both physical and economic capital to support the business. These ethnic firms can also contribute to the community by providing opportunities for workers who cannot fare well in the open economy. In this scenario, linguistic isolation does not restrict business interaction; an individual who lacks fluency in the language of the host society can still conduct economic transactions and observe normal social practices while working within the ethnic economy (Portes and Zhou 1992). Immigrant economies specialize in a few industries where ethnic firms enjoy a competitive advantage, for example in the garment industry in Los Angeles (Waldinger et al 1990).

Ethnic economies increase the potential that previously existing skills, education, and training will be valued in ethnic firms (Bailey and Waldinger 1991). Because ethnic businesses generally do not possess the internal training structures that exist in the primary sector, some ethnic workers must move from firm to firm in order to get ahead (Bailey and Waldinger 1991; Nee et al 1994). However, the strength of ethnic ties may help to compensate both the ethnic bosses and the immigrant workers for their losses. By using a co-ethnic network to hire workers, ethnic bosses can create and sustain a more stable and loyal workforce than their secondary labor market counterparts. Along the same lines, immigrant workers are rewarded over time as their ethnic networks expand job contacts and improve their prospects for gaining skills through a series of jobs[10] (Nee et al 1994; Bailey and Waldinger 1991). Thus, the demand side perspective of immigrant adaptation highlights ethnicities in both finding and filling a job. These arguments are summarized in Hypothesis 4.

H4. Worker's social and economic attainment varies directly with occupational placement. Individuals who work in ethnically concentrated industries receive lower wages than those who work in integrated industries (Labor Market Context).

The ecological and individual theories of immigration outlined above offer different pictures of immigrant adaptation and persistent ethnic inequality. The effects of individual resources and liabilities and of the wider social context on individual and collective immigrant success provide competing explanations for the variation in immigrant attainment. I will combine ideas from both perspectives to show how variation in the skills and origins of contemporary immigrants and the types of areas in which they settle affect their assimilation into the American economy and society.

A MULTILEVEL PERSPECTIVE

The research and analysis I present combines ideas about human and social capital with local labor market conditions. It extends earlier analyses by examining these variables and captures the separate and joint effects of these factors. I analyze immigrant stratification by assessing the co-variation of social and economic attainment and ethnic background. The environment immigrants enter, either dense with ethnic and entrepreneurial ties, or more open with fewer ties, also structures the returns to the individual resources immigrants carry. The current conditions of immigration necessitate this type of research since

---

[10] Nee et al (1994) argue that over the course of an individual's work history, job transitions change from ethnic to non-ethnic in content and informal to formal in terms of market power. As social networks expand through interaction in a mixed economy and the immigrant gains locally valued skills, the probability of working for a co-ethnic decreases. Individuals continually look for jobs with higher returns and more formal labor agreements. This results in movement away from small ethnic firms and toward jobs in the open-formal quadrant.

the newest arrivals carry with them a wider range of resources that, when interjected into different receiving contexts, may result in varying degrees of attainment. Contemporary research must examine how both individual level resources and ecological structures shape the immigrant experience.

The Importance of Social Context

Both individual and family level resources are important to immigrant attainment because many factors contribute to the economic placement of individuals and families i.e., education, marital status, the presence of older adults in the household, ethnicity, and fertility. At the individual level, higher levels of skills, education, and facility with English are associated with higher levels of achievement in terms of occupational placement and income (Mincer 1974). Although their rewards to investments in human capital may be delayed for some time because they are not valued in the local market, individuals eventually accrue experience working in the U.S. so that the benefits to their human capital investments are ultimately redeemed (Goldthorpe 1980). Experience in a local labor market helps potential employers reevaluate foreign credentials.

Additionally, the family can provide a wealth of resources for the immigrant worker, ranging from a source of emotional support to providing a source of unpaid labor for a family business, or by pooling money from several generations of workers for the well-being of the entire family (Sanders and Nee 1996). However, the presence of young children in a household may limit the work force participation of some family members, especially women. The presence of older children or extended family, such as grandparents, may help to offset this deficit as they can care for the younger children and allow more family members to work. Also, there is a tendency for newly arrived families to subordinate individual needs for the greater needs of the family. For example, immigrant entrepreneurship is often made possible through the combined efforts of the family: adults run the business, older grandparents care for younger children, while the adolescents provide unpaid family labor. In this way, the family serves as the social basis for rational economic action (economic attainment in this case).

The social and economic context where the foreign-born find work provides the next link in this analysis. Traditionally, immigrants have been concentrated in specific geographic areas, mainly in "gateway" cities like New York City or Los Angeles and usually in smaller proportions elsewhere (Freeman and Abowd 1990). In fact, the overwhelming majority of immigrants live in just a few cities: New York City, Los Angeles, Chicago, Miami, San Diego, and Houston (*Statistical Abstracts* 1995). Although many native-born individuals blame immigrants for the economic decline of cities in the Northeast and the Midwest, immigrants may be partly responsible for rebuilding and restructuring those cities (Moore 1994). Immigration to these Immigrant Metropolis cities has actually offset the out-migration of native workers who have moved to wealthier suburbs, and this may have bolstered the economy in such cities. In fact, immigration and economic growth correlate positively in many communities. During the past two decades, however, economic restructuring and corporate downsizing have altered mobility paths and some recent immigrants as well as native-born workers may face harsher social environments.

This study examines the mechanisms of opportunity for social mobility within two types of urban contexts, Immigrant Metropolis cities and Regional Centers. The Immigrant Metropolis cities, more globally and ethnically heterogeneous,[11] have larger mixed economies than the Regional Centers. An ethnically heterogeneous urban economy creates opportunities for inter-ethnic ties between individuals as the exchange of resources, services, labor, and commodities bridge the gap between ethnic and non-ethnic communities. Some of the larger cities have many international business connections that promote ethnic diversity in the workforce. Under these conditions of ethnic heterogeneity, connections across ethnic boundaries flourish. Links between non-familiar individuals provide greater sources of information about jobs by cutting across various dimensions of the labor market (Granovetter 1973). Based on the assumption of random mixing of the population, the more a population consists of different cultures and ethnicities, the more opportunities those groups will have for inter-group contact (Blau 1984). Although ethnic solidarity may increase the distinctiveness of certain groups in the short term, labor force heterogeneity may promote inter-group contact, lower long-term

---

[11] Heterogeneity is defined as the extent of differentiation of the members of a collectivity into smaller groups (Blau 1977).

conflict, and relay information about better jobs, ultimately raising the starting wage for ethnics.

An ethnically heterogeneous economy, one with active ethnic economies, produces ties across social class (worker and boss) as well as across ethnic groups (ethnic entrepreneur and consumer) through the exchange of resources and commodities. To this end, social networks are more likely to connect different ethnic groups and provide strong channels (weak ties) for information to flow in heterogeneous economies (Granovetter 1985). Social ties are also important in building solidarity within a multi-ethnic community (Young 1993; Portes and Sensenbrenner 1993). In this manner, competition and conflict may be reduced or overcome. Furthermore, ties that connect low status individuals to individuals of higher status are fundamental to economic opportunities (Lin 1982). In order to find better paying jobs, immigrants must crosscut their traditional and familiar circles to gain information about opportunities outside their community. More clearly, workers use personal ties to learn important facts about their new communities, such as finding a place to live and obtaining jobs. As the amount of time spent in the U.S. increases, the chance that personal ties will cross ethnic and social class boundaries also increases. These ties may eventually connect the immigrant with information that leads him/her to employment outside the confines of an ethnic market. Ultimately, this labor market heterogeneity should initiate a blurring of ethnic boundaries after the initial competitive conflict and hostility subsides.

Historically, economic conditions in the U.S. have shaped social and economic attainment; the idea that the characteristics of the U.S. economy and the social landscape of cities should affect immigrants is not new. To date, there have been at least four major waves of immigration to the U.S.: the Northern and Western Europeans in the mid-nineteenth century; the South Central and Eastern Europeans in the late nineteenth and early twentieth centuries; the migration of black Americans, Mexicans, and Puerto Ricans in the mid-twentieth century; and the post-1965 wave of Latin Americans and Asians.[12] Not only is each period of immigration characterized by an ethnically distinct

---

[12] See Muller and Espendshade (1985) for a full description.

composition, but it is also distinguished by the changing receiving context of the larger U.S. economy for each group.

The first European immigrants who settled in the U.S. entered an agrarian economy, while the second (1830s -1880s) and third (1890s-1920s) waves arrived at a time of industrial expansion. All three of these historical contexts demanded a large surplus of cheap laborers, so that the low wage needs of the agrarian and metropolitan areas were continually replenished by the successive waves of immigration. These unskilled immigrants formed dense ethnic communities close to the centers of employment. They assimilated into the U.S. socially and economically after several generations of workers progressively moved through the ranks of the job queue. The assimilationist perspective and the ideology of the melting pot draw heavily from the experience of these groups, but do not account for the fact that a substantial amount of the social mobility that occurred in times of industrial expansion was structural.[13] That is, individuals attained higher status occupations than their parents simply because the number of higher status jobs increased through structural expansion. A major part of this job shift involved a decline in farming jobs and an increase in technical or skilled positions.

The latest wave of immigrants to the U.S. has arrived in a post-industrial service economy, armed with a broad range of skills and abilities that set them apart from their predecessors. Their assimilation strategies reflect their diversity. Immigrants from countries with expanding technical and service economies come prepared for jobs in those types of labor markets, with English language familiarity and high educational levels. Conversely, immigrants from more agricultural nations are not as prepared. The current demands on the labor pool are more stringent, such that those who arrive with technical skills fare better than those who lack such abilities. Individuals who settle in large globally oriented cities with large ethnic workforces face a different labor market than those who enter a more homogenous economy. During this contemporary period of technological and

---

[13] Structural mobility refers to mobility that occurs because of an expansion of high level positions in the job queue due to economic growth. It contrasts with exchange mobility in which high status positions are created by the vacancy of positions. No new positions are added in an exchange system (Lipset and Bendix 1966).

service expansion and manufacturing and industrial decline, the effect of entering a globally oriented city as compared to a smaller nationally centered city on immigrant assimilation is a point of departure for this study.

The U.S. economy, although still the world's largest, has declined in its share of total global output over the past 20 years (Ford Foundation 1993). No longer dominated by the steel, coal, and iron industries, the American economy has contracted at the lowest occupational tier, which has resulted in fewer positions for unskilled labor. The shifts in consumer spending from goods to services along with the major reduction in national defense spending brought on by the end of the Cold War have had profound implications for national employment patterns. Employment has declined in real numbers in most goods producing sectors and in many blue-collar occupations. This occupational contraction has most seriously affected racial and ethnic minorities, because they are often concentrated in many of these declining industries (Bluestone and Harrison 1982). New demands for labor exist mainly in the service sector and in metropolitan areas, mainly in occupations that have replaced the need for physical strength with automation and instead emphasize intellectual abilities and interpersonal communication. This requires that immigrants today must rely on several modes of attainment. Those modes of attainment ultimately shape their mobility patterns. Individuals who enter low end or traditional occupations filled by immigrants enter a system characterized primarily by exchange mobility. On the other hand, the high-tech sector has high rates of structural mobility due to its rapid expansion. Those who enter the traditional way are more likely to experience high mobility only if they shift to a different and expanding occupational sector.

The urban labor market is currently highly stratified in terms of wages and the organization of work. In general, the overall shift from a manufacturing to a service economy has opened up white collar employment opportunities at the expense of blue collar employment. Nevertheless, it is erroneous to ignore the impact of the manufacturing sector on immigrants, since these industries still wield employment power (Scott 1985). Low skill workers do find manufacturing jobs in the informal economy, albeit marginal employment often in sweatshops (Sassen 1988). Ironically, the evolution of many urban

centers into globally connected centers of international trade and finance
has increased labor market stratification. Under the pressure of global
competition, many large firms have either restructured or eliminated
middle level jobs (Scott 1985; Stanback and Noyell 1982), leaving
highly paid managers working along side low wage laborers.

UNITING COMPETING MODELS OF ATTAINMENT:
A THEORETICAL SYNTHESIS

Each of the above frameworks outlines a specific explanation for
immigrant stratification. In the first, individual credentials and
resources determine a worker's position the labor market. In contrast,
the contextual arguments emphasize the features of the host society that
govern immigrant social and economic attainment outcomes. In this
analysis, I combine elements from economics of discrimination, human
and social capital, and local labor market conditions to extend these
theories and to offer a more complete picture of the social and
economic stratification of contemporary U.S. immigrants. Similar to
Lieberson (1980) and Glazer and Moynihan (1963) this research
examines social and economic factors that lead to ethnic stratification
between several different immigrant groups. Variation in skills,
resources, and strategies for attainment combine with discrimination
and the ecological factors of the host city and ultimately create different
modes of social and economic attainment. Although these three
competing arguments explain ethnic differences in attainment, they
may not be mutually exclusive, and in fact, may have both indirect and
direct effects on attainment.

Figure 2.1 diagrams the arguments I describe above. The figure
depicts the direct effects that ethnic discrimination, human and social
capital processes, and local labor market characteristics have on income
and occupational attainments. The directed arrows reproduce
predictions of Hypotheses 1, 2, 3, and 4. The limitations of census
data do not permit me to estimate the direct effects of wage and job
discrimination. I draw upon an alternate strategy for this argument and
use Figure 2.2 to describe it.

The arrows that connect ethnicity, human and social capital, and
local labor market conditions to attainment outcomes represent the
zero-order effects in Figure 2.1. In Figure 2.2, those paths represent the
direct effects of the relevant factors net of the effects of other processes.

Figure 2.1: Direct Effects in Immigrant Attainment Model

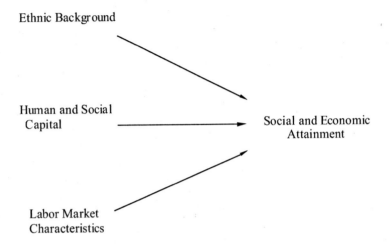

Figure 2.2: Immigrant Attainment Model, As Tested

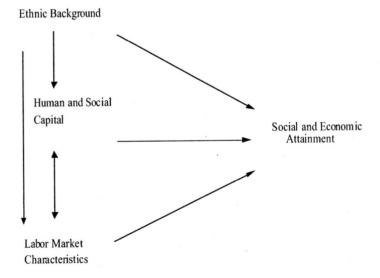

As an example, personal resources index the financial and social capital immigrants use to negotiate income and positions in the labor market. Those factors are presumed to affect income and occupational status independent of ethnic discrimination or local labor market factors. If ethnic differences in attainment are due solely to ethnic differences on human and social capital factors, the relationship between ethnicity and outcome measures should fall to zero. Human and social capital arguments (H2) explain all of the ethnic variation in attainments. On the other hand, human and social capital processes may only explain part of the ethnic differences in attainments. The residual ethnic effect, while not demonstrating evidence of discrimination, is consistent with a discrimination argument. Under such circumstances, one can claim that human and social capital processes account for an identifiable component of ethnic differences in attainment and that the residual ethnic effect may be due to the effects of discrimination and other unmeasured factors.

I argue that an analysis that combines ethnic heritage, human and social capital factors and local labor market resources builds on the traditional ways of viewing immigrant attainment. In this study, I use the type of city an immigrant enters, i.e., Immigrant Metropolis cities or Regional Centers, and the degree of ethnic concentration of owners and workers to classify the local context. I use city-level indicators because the social and economic environment within a country is not constant. With credentials valued in their homeland but rewarded inconsistently in the U.S., foreign-born individuals depend heavily on the economic and social institutions they encounter upon their arrival. One source of variation in immigrant experiences may be the ways that human capital factors are rewarded in local labor markets. Abilities along with opportunities place individuals in local labor markets. Capital accumulated and valued in a different cultural context, is re-evaluated and converted into meaningful resources in the new environment. Individual characteristics that may affect attainment outcomes directly also affect occupational trajectories based on their value in local labor markets and city contexts. Individual position in the labor market varies directly with the individual level resources. Ultimately these positions in the labor market affect individual social and economic attainment. Higher status jobs in the open economy provide better financial rewards to the immigrants who are able to secure them (H3).

The economic context that the immigrants enter is important in another way. The larger more ethnically diverse and internationally linked Immigrant Metropolis cities contrast with the smaller more ethnically homogenous and nationally oriented Regional Centers. Individual level characteristics influence where the immigrant will work, in an open or an ethnic economy. This occupational placement in turn shapes social and economic attainment (H4). Hence the integration of personal, ethnic, and family resources along with the local labor market conditions delineates a revised view of contemporary immigrant stratification.

To examine this new urban transformation, I focus on metropolitan areas linked to the global economy and compare them with smaller urban regional centers. As worldwide competition has given the American economy a larger scope, a small number of global cities have come to dominate the international business landscape (Scott 1985; Ohmae 1990). The trend for internationalization results in part from an increase in multinational corporate headquarters, international banking, and international trade and finance concentrated in key "global" cities. The role of major cities as producers and exporters of specialized services reflects the technological changes of work, as witnessed by the growth of the financial sector and the transnationalization of capital (Ohmae 1990). These are large, formerly industrial cities with a broad base for low skill labor and expanding technological and service sectors to support a growing professional and managerial class. To this end, the growth of high-income jobs accompanies the increase of very low-income jobs (Sassen 1988). This growing stratification is linked directly to the emergence of an integrated world economy with transnational market opportunities and international borders. In terms of economics, international relations have taken precedence with the advent of a single European market and NAFTA which further reduce the importance of national borders and emphasize a global economy (Edwards and Garrona 1991).

The labor market of each metropolitan area, global or domestic based, is a mix of employment systems. The range and importance of the main industries not only determines the organization of work but also influences the layout of the transportation systems and residential areas (Hiestand and Morse 1979). Highly skilled positions exist along side jobs that require no training. For every professional job in a high-rise office building, there are many lower skill jobs required to make sure that position runs smoothly, e.g., cleaning staff, mail services, and security. Additionally, the declining industrial sectors and the informal economy demand a continual supply of cheap labor for economic survival, which is provided by the streams of new immigrants. Large numbers of foreign-born seek employment in these industrial and service centers. In these heterogeneous economic and social orders, immediate assimilation is not demanded so that ethnic communities continue to thrive.

Many ethnic workers draw on information provided by their fellow ethnics to find employment. These ethnic job networks often link the low skill, linguistically isolated immigrants to jobs in ethnically concentrated industries. Following this reasoning, in cities where there are larger proportions of immigrants, there will be more industries that are ethnically concentrated. The greater this ethnic industry concentration, the more likely that individual foreign-born ethnics will spend at least part of their occupational careers there. However, the more ethnically heterogeneous the city is, the higher the random chance of association between ethnics and non-ethnics, and thus the larger the size and number of ethnic enterprises and the more even dispersal of immigrants throughout the job queue.

The general pattern of labor market stratification heavily influences immigrant stratification. Instead of following one path toward economic assimilation, new entrants may be better characterized as following one of two paths – the traditional "J" curve[14] or the contemporary accelerated path. Both modes of attainment are shaped by the economic and social climate of the receiving context and both reflect the skills the immigrants possess. The first, similar to the historic path, is that of the laborer who possesses menial levels of educational and occupational skills, who holds no prior entrepreneurial experience, and whose greatest asset is physical strength. This individual finds employment in the lowest occupational tier in industry or agriculture and is most similar to the earlier waves of immigrants.

---

[14] The immigration curve reflects the amount of time it takes individuals to recoup losses in status from the transition from the homeland to the U.S. Usually there is an initial decline, which is followed by upward mobility across successive generations. See Goldthorpe (1980) for a full description.

Eventually, the second or third generation of this family is able to work their way up the occupational queue. Conversely, the second mode of attainment exists mainly for the newest waves of immigrant professionals. This group brings with them high levels of educational and technical occupational skills, money accumulated in their homeland, and occasionally some small business experience. With such mixes of types of capital, this group can find employment throughout the technical and professional levels of the job queue. By "leapfrogging" over jobs in the downgraded industries, these immigrants and their families experience relatively rapid social and economic attainment. Therefore, contemporary immigrants may find initial occupational placement throughout the occupational structure.

Because of the changes in the diversity of immigrants who enter the U.S. and the fluid institutional context into which they settle, this study examines the effect of four levels of independent variables – ethnic heritage, human and social capital, local labor market indicators, and the full model on social and economic attainment. The traditional focus on immigrant credentials and skills or labor market structures as the dominant forces governing individual mobility by themselves present an incomplete picture of the complex process of the social and economic stratification of contemporary immigrants. By combining both views, this study builds on individual and family level resources and embeds them within an ecological framework. The different origins from which contemporary immigrants come and the changing economic and social structures of the U.S. cities they enter necessitate a new approach to immigrant stratification. Both low skill and more technically skilled immigrants enter leading metropolitan areas and encounter different paths toward social and economic well-being. In summary, this research tests hypotheses drawn from several different theories simultaneously with different populations living in different locales. By linking ethnic background, social institutional factors, and personal capital resources, this offers a contemporary and more complete view of the social and economic attainment of the foreign-born into the U.S.

CHAPTER 3:
Background and Description of Study

This chapter outlines the research design for the immigrant attainment model introduced in Chapter 2. It describes some of the newest groups to arrive in the U.S., provides background on the changes in their U.S. metropolitan destinations, and presents the approach to data analysis. The model focuses on the effects of ethnic background, human and social capital, and local labor market experiences on social on economic attainment for Asians and Latin Americans, the two largest groups that comprise contemporary immigration. Their experiences are compared to foreign-born non-Hispanic whites, the immigrant group most culturally similar to the native-born white population. I have selected five specific ethnic groups to study: Chinese, Filipino, Korean, Cuban, and Mexican immigrants.[15] I describe the effects of ethnic differences for immigrant groups often treated as one large ethnic group, i.e., Asians or Hispanics. I also consider differences in the principal destination cities. I contrast Immigrant Metropolis cities (Los Angeles, Miami, and New York City), large international hubs, with Regional Centers (Atlanta and Denver), smaller domestic cities, in order to examine the effects of variation in local labor market conditions on immigrant attainment.

Preceding the research design, I present short histories of the immigration experiences of each group as well as a general

---

[15]The groups are listed alphabetically within each larger category of Asian and Hispanic.

description of the five cities in the study. The historical descriptions illuminate the key aspects of ethnic stratification that frame the increased contemporary immigration to these cities. I conclude the chapter with a description of the study design, data, and indicators.

IMMIGRANT GROUP BACKGROUND
Chinese Immigration

Compared with the other Asian groups in this study, Chinese immigrants have the longest history of settlement in the U.S. Trade between China and the Philippines, an early Spanish colony, exposed Chinese sailors to travel to the New World as early as the 18th century. By the time America gained independence, Chinese sailors were a common sight on western ships (Mangiafico 1988). Although small numbers of Chinese were recorded living in Pennsylvania in 1785 (Daniels 1988) and in Connecticut in 1818 (Mangiafico 1988), the majority of Chinese immigrants came to the U.S. in the years following the gold rushes of the West.[16] Specifically, the Gold Rush of 1848 initiated an increase in the Chinese population, so that from 1850-1882, there were approximately 300,000 immigrants living in western states (Daniels 1988). The vast majority of these immigrants were young male sojourners, such that the sex ratio for this group was quite skewed, with men outnumbering women by more than twenty-to-one (Daniels 1990; Takaki 1987).

During this period, most European immigrants to the U.S. found laboring jobs along the East coast closest to the ports into which they first arrived. True to this pattern, Asian immigrants also remained close to their port of entry. However, instead of entering the U.S. through Ellis Island, these immigrants arrived in the West through Angel Island in San Francisco Bay. The job opportunities they found on the West coast were confined mainly to mining, agriculture, and transportation. Many laborers were bound by illegal indentures that forced them to work in the mines or on the railroads for an indeterminate period to pay for their journey to the U.S. American industrialists frequently used Chinese workers to undercut white labor,

---

[16] California was known to many Chinese immigrants as "Gold Mountain" because of the stories of its wealth that circulated in China.

which often led to outbreaks of violence against the immigrants along the lines of a split labor market (Takaki 1987).

Native-born workers did not openly discriminate against Chinese workers at first. However, once these immigrants began to stake their own claims in the gold fields, they increasingly encountered resistance from white miners, who forced them into mining areas already abandoned by others. Once the "gold fever" subsided, some Chinese laborers found employment working on the transcontinental railroad. Because this work was difficult, dangerous, meagerly paid, and otherwise undesirable, Chinese immigrants met with little job resistance from native-born white workers.

Some scholars attribute the resurgence of nativism in the middle of the 19th century to the expansion of immigration throughout the 1850s and the growing uncertainty about the future of the newly reunited U.S. in the 1860s. Although naturalization was broadened to include persons of African descent along with white persons after the Civil War, Asians were explicitly excluded and categorized as "aliens ineligible for citizenship." The immigration legislation of this period sought to protect American labor from competition from the growing numbers of unskilled immigrant workers arriving in the U.S. Recently freed slaves and a weak Southern economy further fueled fears of job competition from both blacks and foreign-born workers.

After completion of the transcontinental railroad, many Chinese workers found jobs in California's and Hawaii's agricultural sectors, clearing swamps and planting and harvesting fruit and vegetables for the new migrants from the East coast. The rapid influx of new Californians also initiated a need for many service businesses such as laundries, restaurants, clothing stores, and general construction, a niche quickly filled by Chinese entrepreneurs. Even in these occupations typically associated with Chinese workers, they faced discrimination. Although comprising less than 10% of California's total population, Chinese workers represented over 25% of the workforce (Mangiafico 1988), which exacerbated the frustration of native workers during the economic depression of the 1880s and resulted in open hostility toward Chinese workers.

The late 19th century brought about the first institutionalized immigration policies of exclusion targeted at a specific ethnic group. After sixty years of importing cheap manual laborers, U.S. labor leaders lobbied for restrictions on Chinese immigration. Ironically, immigration during this time period was overwhelmingly European. The resulting Chinese Exclusion Act of 1882 was thinly disguised as a general labor protective strategy. It restricted the future arrival of Chinese laborers, but allowed small numbers of Chinese merchants and other privileged individuals continued entry. Although the original term of the policy was ten years, Congress renewed it in 1892 and subsequently incorporated it into U.S. immigration policy as a permanent restriction. The National Quota Acts of the 1920s halted Chinese immigration entirely.

Because China was a U.S. ally during World War II, the Chinese Exclusion Act was withdrawn in 1943. Chinese residents were also granted naturalization at this time, if desired, and the long-standing exclusionist policy was replaced with a token quota for Chinese immigrants of 105 per year (Daniels 1990; Yang 1995). After the 1965 immigration reform, the numbers of Chinese immigrating to the U.S. increased substantially. In particular, Asian immigrants have utilized immigration preferences for family members, refugees, and occupational skills in order to gain admittance to the U.S. (Yang 1995). This resurgence in Chinese entry revitalized the previously existing Chinese American communities, 96.5% of which are located in metropolitan areas (Mangiafico 1988) where the new arrivals can find work, build on ethnic networks, and seek out other co-ethnics.

While many contemporary Chinese Americans have high incomes and education, there is evidence of an increase in stratification between those individuals who are fully integrated into the mainstream and those who are only marginally employed. The Chinese foreign-born community is characterized by many contradictions, such as large numbers of college educated along with many who have little schooling, many in top managerial positions and many who are unemployed, many who are fully acculturated and still more who cannot speak English. The bifurcation of the Chinese American community challenges the notion of a "Model Minority" since the "silent" Chinese immigrants, the unemployed and poverty-stricken, form a sizable group (Daniels 1990; Farley 1996). In all probability, Chinese immigration will increase, but the future of this group's internal stratification is unclear.

Korean immigration

In 1882, the U.S. established one of the first western trade and friendship treaties with Korea (Wong 1986). Over the next two decades, many Koreans immigrated to Hawaii to fill a void left by Chinese workers on the sugar and pineapple plantations (Takaki 1987). Like the Chinese immigrants before them, the Korean immigrants were mostly young men seeking their fortune in the U.S. However, in 1905, the Korean government stopped all immigration to the U.S. because of complaints concerning their treatment by U.S. employers (Mangiafico 1988). Many Korean laborers circumvented this law by migrating first to Hawaii and then to the mainland. President Theodore Roosevelt stopped this practice with the 1907 *Gentleman's Agreement* (Takaki 1989). This restriction did not, however, apply to Korean picture-brides, women who contracted marriage to fellow ethnics already living in the U.S. on the basis of exchange of letters and pictures. This marriage practice grew rapidly because of the high number of single Korean men already living in the U.S. Between 1910 and 1924, more than 1,000 of these women entered the U.S. to join their new spouses (Mangiafico 1988). This produced a more even sex ratio within the Korean community than in the Chinese immigrant communities of that period.

Because many Korean immigrants were urban and literate before their emigration, they did not remain on the sugar plantations for long. Indeed, many left to seek out better paying employment in urban areas both in Hawaii and on the mainland. They fell into the economic niches that are now typically associated with Korean immigrants and worked as tailors, shopkeepers, or restaurateurs. Entry into professional occupations was essentially barred, given that Asian naturalization was still forbidden by law. The National Origins Quotas Acts of the 1920s curtailed Korean immigration for the next two decades.

After the end of the Korean War in 1954, many more Korean women came to the U.S. as brides of U.S. servicemen. However, as with other Asian groups, large-scale Korean immigration only began after the 1965 immigration reforms. Individuals who possessed occupational skills valued by U.S. employers were given preference for entry. Most Korean immigrants in this group were under 40 years of age, from the middle class, and highly educated. Hailing from the very top levels of the labor force, these skilled workers gained much from moving abroad, namely economic prosperity at a relatively rapid pace. Their command of income and resources quickly permitted them to overcome many barriers in the U.S. (Edwards and Garrona 1991). Additional categories of Korean entrants to the U.S. have included small groups of students, relatives of U.S. citizens, and Korean children adopted by U.S. parents (Daniels 1990).

One distinguishing feature of Korean immigrants is the prominent number of entrepreneurs. These entrepreneurs fill a niche left open by U.S. businessmen. They serve an ethnic clientele in retail and service sectors (e.g., fruit stands, grocery stores, service stations, and liquor stores) often located in high-risk low income neighborhoods. These small businesses do not generally cater to other Koreans, but rather to other minorities, and provide services as a typical "middleman minority." The ethnic antagonism they often experience may result from their intermediary position in the labor market.[17]

Filipino immigration

In the late 19th century, small numbers of Filipinos, like the Koreans years before, immigrated to Hawaii and California to work in the agricultural sector. However, the turn of the century brought the first sizable groups of legal Filipino immigrants to the U.S. Some came as students, while others came as workers for the sugar plantations in Hawaii. Most of this population was comprised of young Catholic men who took up the agricultural work left by the Chinese and Korean laborers who came before them. Some U.S. employers viewed them as a cheap and docile labor force, and since they were American nationals due to the outcome of the Spanish American war of 1898, no quotas restricted their immigration. However, they, like all other Asians in the U.S., were categorized as aliens ineligible for citizenship.

By the middle 1920s, Filipinos represented 50% of the plantation workers in Hawaii, a figure that grew to 75% by the next decade (Mangiafico 1988). Many immigrants had prior contact with American culture because of their education in schools run by Americans in the Philippines, such that their new home was not as alien to them as it

---

[17]The 1992 riots in Los Angeles in which Korean merchants experienced the brunt of ethnic violence and destruction are case in point.

was to other Asian groups. The nature and transience of seasonal work caused many Filipino migrants to disperse in urban areas rather than form cohesive enclave communities. Although they faced high levels of resistance and discrimination, Filipinos were protected from deportation by U.S. law. As U.S. nationals, Filipinos were not subject to the 1920s immigration quotas. When the Tydings-McDuffie Act of 1935 promised independence to the Philippines, it classified Filipino immigrants as aliens, and thus considerably reduced their ability to legally immigrate to the U.S.[18] Over the next two decades, Filipino immigration exceeded its annual quota, as many individuals were granted entry under the McCarren-Walter family provisions in 1952 (Daniels 1990).

Contemporary Filipino immigrants have entered the U.S. in larger numbers than Chinese and Korean immigrants by utilizing service and technical occupational preference categories in medicine and computer technology that have priority in the new immigration laws. However, they have not settled in dense ethnic neighborhoods like other Asian immigrants; there are no substantial Manillatowns like the Koreatowns or Chinatowns that still exist in many large cities. Prior exposure to American culture may again be the main reason for this lack of ethnic residential solidarity. These new entrants frequently have encountered licensing barriers to the transfer of their skills, which has delayed their immediate assimilation. However, they have not followed the same path as Korean immigrants toward self-employment. Filipino immigrants tended initially to take lower prestige jobs for which they were overqualified. Once they accumulated job experience in the U.S. they were able to find better paying jobs. Most likely, high levels of Filipino immigration will continue in the future, as the Filipino population in the U.S. has obtained high levels of economic success.

Cuban immigration

Cuban immigration to the U.S. provides a striking contrast to the immigration of Mexican nationals and other Latin Americans. The reception of Cubans as political refugees as compared to the reception of Mexican economic migrants underscores the different experience of

---

[18]Fifty individuals were eligible for entrance per year (Wong 1986). This figure doubled in 1946 as the U.S. made concessions to its wartime allies.

the two groups.[19]   Similar to Mexican immigrants, the roots of immigration for Cubans are embedded in U.S. geopolitical relations. However, unlike Mexican immigrants, many Cubans were not pulled to the U.S. by economic motivation, but rather were pushed by political unrest in Cuba. Furthermore, their immigration to the U.S. has been one-way, with an absence of return flows to Cuba.

Cuban migration to the U.S. is a relatively recent phenomenon, especially in comparison to the immigration histories of the other groups in this study. Prior to the 1960s, fewer than 50,000 Cubans lived in the U.S. Fidel Castro's takeover in 1959 initiated the first exodus of Cuban émigrés. Along with Fulgencio Bastista's flight from power came the massive departure of landowners, industrialists, and professionals. Close to 250,000 members of the affluent professional class left the island at this time (Portes and Bach 1985). As the U.S. and Cuba negotiated a formal immigration policy, the number of exiles quickly grew.

The 1962 crisis surrounding the placement of Russian missiles in Cuba halted all flights to the U.S. and temporarily stopped the flow of immigration. However, in 1965, Castro permitted individuals who had family already living in the U.S. to leave. Subsequently, an airlift brought another 350,000 Cubans seeking asylum to the U.S. (Portes and Bach 1985). Most settled in the Miami area. Over the next two years, Cuba and the U.S. negotiated several other airlifts, but all flights were halted in 1973.

In 1980, Cuba opened the port of Mariel to anyone who wanted to leave. The subsequent sealift brought another 125,000 Cuban refugees to the U.S. (Card 1990). Many debates surround the class status of these exiles. Although they were less skilled and not as well educated as the earlier migrants, they had more human capital than the general population of Cuba at that time. Most of those immediately released into the Miami community had relatives in the area and were thus able to integrate quickly into the Cuban American community. Of the remainder

---

[19] Although the fate of recent Cuban immigrants to the U.S. has yet to be determined, it will be interesting to study whether their assimilation will follow the path of Cubans already living in the U.S. as political refugees, or of Mexicans as economic migrants. Their situation is readily compared to both.

placed directly into U.S. refugee camps, many were single non-whites with a history of incarceration (Portes and Bach 1985). These individuals were not as easily incorporated into the community. Differences in their skills and criminal records created barriers to assimilation and resulted in growing stratification within the U.S. Cuban community. The "open arms" policy of receiving Cuban immigrants halted in the early 1990s, with the increase in Cubans fleeing Cuba by raft (Grenier and Pérez 1996). The U.S. began to intercept these vessels at sea and sent the passengers to refugee camps without hope of entering the U.S.

The first cohort of Cuban exiles created a strong ethnic economy in the Miami area. Many individuals experienced significant economic and occupational mobility after a relatively short period of adjustment. The strong economic and social institutions this group created may have eased the transition at least in part for the Mariel group. By entering a strong Cuban American economy, the later groups have had a different experience than those who immigrated earlier.

Mexican immigration

Much like Asian immigration, the relationship the U.S. developed with Mexican immigrants is deeply entrenched in labor protectionist ideology. Immigration from Mexico originated with the deliberate recruitment of cheap Mexican labor by North American companies throughout the 19th century, and, until the 20th century, the flow of Mexican labor across the border was outside the control of the U.S. government (Grebler, Moore, and Guzman 1979). Because of the difficulty in regulating the national border and the unstable political climate caused by the Mexican Revolution in 1910, the number of Mexicans traveling to and residing in the U.S. increased dramatically during the 20th century.

Historically, the flow of Mexican migration and immigration, as well as U.S. attempts to control the national border, have depended on the state of the American economy. As the needs of American industry expanded, low wage Mexican workers crossed the border to find work. For example, after the economic and political upheavals in Mexico in 1909 and the economic expansion in the U.S. in the years that followed, many Mexicans sought employment and refuge in the U.S.[20] In doing so, they alleviated the labor shortages in the Southwest caused in part by the restriction on Asian immigration. The needs of the growing agricultural economy in the West and demands of assembly line work in the Northeast required large amounts of low wage labor. Mexican workers filled this need and were welcomed by the American public at this time. This response changed with the onset of the Great Depression, when several hundred thousand Mexicans were expelled from the U.S. Only then, in a time of economic contraction, did crossing the border to the U.S. become illegal. After the labor shortages caused by the onset of World War II, the border with Mexico relaxed and permitted relatively easy crossing. The Bracero program, instituted in 1942, encouraged the seasonal migration of large numbers of Mexican agricultural workers.[21] However, in the 1950s, as the migration of Mexicans again concerned the American public, the federal government initiated "Operation Wetback" to forcibly expel Mexicans from the U.S. In 1954 alone, the U.S. government removed over one million Mexicans, many of whom were, in fact, U.S. citizens (Massey 1986).

Social networks of personal ties, which were less costly to employers, soon replaced the official worker-employer networks established by the Bracero program (Massey 1986). Bosses trusted Mexican contacts to provide reliable workers, most often relatives or friends, to fill labor needs. Information about jobs thus easily bypassed the Bracero recruitment centers and flowed directly into the sending communities in Mexico (Massey et al 1994).

The tremendous scale of Mexican immigration today is based on the development of the social networks that initially created it. The social networks continue to sponsor seasonal migration, both legal and illegal, of family and friends of those who have already worked in the

---

[20] Like all Western Hemisphere countries, Mexico was exempt from the National Origins Acts of 1921 and 1924.

[21] Under this program, U.S. government officials traveled to Mexico to recruit agricultural laborers to work in the U.S. to alleviate wartime labor shortages. American agribusiness was able to extend the program after the war ended to maintain a cheap supply of low wage workers (Portes and Bach 1985).

U.S. Over time, this migration has become self-perpetuating as the economic conditions that originally sparked it no longer exist; yet the border crossings continue due to the strength of the established networks (Massey 1986). The current migration of Mexican workers is largely self-sustaining, since it has become a frequent family strategy to send at least one relative to the U.S. for temporary employment (Massey et al 1994). This individual, usually a son or a brother, works for a season and returns home with his profit.

Some of the latest research on immigration examines the lifecourse of sending communities. Migration to the U.S. tends to increase in frequency as the social capital of migrants, i.e., their knowledge and network connections, grows. Over time, migration becomes a generalized social and economic practice for Mexican communities (Massey, Goldring, and Durand 1994).

Illegal, or undocumented, immigration mirrors the legal flows of immigration. It continues without overt recruitment by North American companies (Portes and Bach 1985). It is clear, however, that some companies do encourage illegal immigration. In contrast to legal immigration, undocumented immigration tends to be more seasonal and temporary. The reported number of migrants varies greatly, depending on the source and can fluctuate between 2 and 12 million people per year. Currently, the generally accepted figure is around 4 million people per year (*Statistical Abstracts* 1995), which may be offset to a large degree by return migration. The Immigration Reform Act of 1986 attempted to deter, or at least control, the scale of undocumented immigration. Essentially, it provided amnesty to those who had been living in the U.S. since 1982 and increased the prosecution of employers who hired illegal immigrants. In California, where the highest concentration of Mexican immigrants reside, the unease with current immigration policy is underscored with recent policy such as Proposition 187 which restricts the social services available to illegal immigrants as well as their children.[22]

---

[22]Specifically the policy "makes illegal aliens ineligible for public social services..., and public school education at elementary, secondary, and post-secondary levels." It also, "requires various state and local agencies to report persons who are suspected illegal aliens to the United States

IMMIGRANT METROPOLIS DESTINATIONS

Immigrants generally have entered the U.S. at key points of entry, then scattered across the country. Typically, Asians entered on the West coast, Europeans arrived in the East coast, and Latin Americans entered along the Southern border. Contemporary changes in the mode of travel has meant that the newest U.S. immigrants still enter at key points, usually the global transportation hubs of New York City, Boston, Chicago, Los Angeles, and Miami. Post-1965 immigrants have chosen just a few areas to live, close to those global hubs, where they are fairly residentially concentrated. In fact, more than two-thirds of new immigrants have settled in just six states: California, New York, Texas, Florida, Illinois, and New Jersey. These new immigrants have chosen mainly metropolitan destinations, as more than 95% reside in urban areas, and over half of them live in center cities (Yang 1995). New York City, Los Angeles, and Miami are among the most popular metropolitan destinations for contemporary immigrants (*Statistical Abstracts* 1990).[23] Large ethnically heterogeneous cities are the main destination for most contemporary immigrants, although a second tier of smaller cities is beginning to attract larger numbers. Together the numbers of foreign-born in Los Angeles and New York City exceed all other *state* populations of foreign-born Americans (Bozorgmehr, Sabagh, and Light 1996).

The economy is the most important factor for the concentration of immigrants in a few select areas. Los Angeles has experienced dramatic growth in terms of job opportunities at all levels of the job queue (Yang 1995) notwithstanding a major recession in the early 1990s. Likewise, the increased trade between Latin American countries and the U.S. has created a new global city in Miami, which has become known as the "capital" of Latin America. Although New York City has experienced industrial decline like other cities in the Northeast, it maintains a strong service sector and many thriving ethnic communities that attract new entrants daily. Existing ethnic networks

---

Immigration and Naturalization Service" (McDonnell (1994) as quoted in Bozorgmehr, Sabagh, and Light 1996).

[23]The top immigrant metropolitan area destinations in 1990 in descending order are: Los Angeles, New York City, Chicago, Houston, Washington D.C., Miami, San Diego, San Francisco, Boston, and Dallas.

draw new immigrants who revitalize ethnic communities. The spatial concentration of fellow ethnics establishes a stable, if not expanding, ethnic economy that provides cultural and social resources for the new immigrant community. Although in some instances immigrants have replaced native workers in low skill jobs, the economic well-being of New York City, Los Angeles, and Miami has been promoted by small business activity for which immigrants are at least partially responsible (U.S. Department of Labor 1989). The dynamics of the local labor markets are key to understanding contemporary ethnic stratification. Since the 1965 revision in immigration law, the Immigrant Metropolis cities of New York City, Los Angeles, and Miami have had relatively strong economic growth.

Los Angeles

Los Angeles has been a major hub of immigrant activity for the past thirty years. In fact, immigrants account for about 70% of the growth in the city's working population since the 1970s (U.S. Department of Labor 1989). Furthermore, 32% of the U.S. foreign-born population resides in the Los Angeles metropolitan area alone (Gall 1995). One out of every four residents in the Los Angeles area is foreign-born (Farley 1996). Although many researchers point to the large immigrant population of Asians and Hispanics as contributing to racial tension in the city, others identify the positive aspects of immigration. Immigrants augment the labor force and often take low-skill jobs in manufacturing that may benefit industries in Los Angeles. Also, the low wage jobs filled by immigrants may translate into lower prices for goods and services for consumers. Los Angeles seems to reflect the diversity of the immigrants who flock to it. Although the question of the total effects of immigration is unresolved, some researchers indicate that the benefits for Los Angeles may outweigh the costs, as economic prosperity may counterbalance the dislocation of native-born workers (Moore 1994).

Miami

Prior to the 1960s, issues between native-born black and white residents dominated race relations in Miami. However, the inflow of Cuban refugees into the Miami area has radically altered the city culture, economy, and ethnic composition. Currently more than 50% of the population claims Hispanic descent and another 23% is composed of either native-born Blacks or individuals from the Caribbean (Grenier and Pérez 1996). In addition, the ratio of foreign-born to native-born individuals is the highest in the country, where more than one out of every three Miami residents is an immigrant (Moore 1994). Although the Mariel boatlift alone increased the Cuban population by 7%, there have been relatively few adverse effects in terms of job dislocation of the native-born. In fact, the Cuban immigrants have rapidly integrated into the Miami labor force with negligible effects on other working groups (Card 1990). Furthermore, Florida's economy, especially in Miami, has benefited tremendously from the influx of Latin American investment funds. The cash flow from illicit drug trafficking and from the reliance upon underpaid immigrant labor to provide many of the services in the area have further added to the economic boom (Gall 1995).

New York City

Like several other large Eastern seaboard cities, New York City has acted as a gateway for numerous waves of immigration for over two centuries and as a destination for large numbers of blacks who left the South after World War I. The city's more than two million immigrants (Moore 1994) have counterbalanced the manufacturing-based and skilled laborers who have fled to the suburbs in the years after World War II. The ethnic economies they revived have improved the overall economic picture of New York City, both small-scale retail and large-scale garment industries. Although New York City is known for its securities industry, banking, communications, and wholesale trade, foreign-born workers generally find employment in the manufacturing or service sectors. As European immigrants appear to have fully integrated into New York City's contemporary political and cultural institutions, African Americans, Asians, and Hispanics have become more important influences in the ethnic relations of the city (Binder and Reimers 1996).

REGIONAL CENTERS

The two Regional Centers in this study, Denver and Atlanta, provide a good comparison to the Immigrant Metropolis cities in terms of size, industry, and racial and ethnic relations. Both Denver and Atlanta have strong regional economies that have recently experienced substantial growth in both the energy and telecommunications industries, which has prompted rapid migration of both native and foreign-born individuals to these areas. They also have sizable minority populations, although they are mostly comprised of native-born individuals. However, if the regional economies continue to expand, growth in their immigrant populations should grow as well.

Atlanta

Atlanta is the commercial, industrial, and financial giant of the Southeast. It is also known as a transportation hub for the area because of its extensive road and rail systems. Industry in Atlanta rivals the Immigrant Metropolis cities since many Fortune 500 companies are headquartered there, including CNN, Coca-Cola, and UPS. In terms of racial and ethnic relations, African Americans form the majority in the Atlanta metropolitan area and represent 67.1% of the population (Gall 1995). Overall, the state of Georgia has a low level of ethnic diversity. Only 2.8% of the state's population are foreign-born (Gall 1995).

Denver

Compared to the Immigrant Metropolis cities in terms of overall population and industrial growth, Denver is quite small with a metropolitan population of less than 2 million. However, close to half of Colorado's population lives in the Denver metropolitan area (Gall 1995). Denver itself is geographically structured like typical western cities with many smaller suburban communities linked into its sprawling metropolis. It is known chiefly as the center for finance and commerce for the West, but is also headquarters for many companies that research and develop known reserves of fossil fuel as well as alternative energy sources. High tech research in telecommunications and manufacturing grew substantially in the 1980s and 1990s which, coupled with rapid growth and an expanding economy, has made this area a popular destination for many U.S. migrants as well as immigrants. In terms of race and ethnic relations, the Hispanic influence on Colorado's history, culture, and economy is of great importance— 23% of Denver residents claim Hispanic descent (Gall 1995).

DATA AND ANALYTICAL PROCEDURES

The data for this study are drawn from the 5% Public Use Microdata Sample (PUMS) 1990 Census data file. The PUMS 5% sample contains household and person records for a sub-sample of housing units that received the "long form" of the 1990 Census, approximately 15.9% of all housing units. This sample comprises over 12 million persons and over 5 million housing units (U.S. Department of Commerce 1990). Each person identified in the sample has an associated household record, which contains data for all persons living in the household and general household characteristics. The clear advantage of using the 5% PUMS data is its size, in that it contains sufficient cases of foreign-born respondents for a critical study of different immigrant populations.

These analyses use data for persons who indicated on the Census that they were born outside the U.S: Asians born in China (Including Taiwan), Korea, or the Philippines and Hispanics born in Cuba or Mexico. The comparison group, all foreign-born non-Hispanic whites living in each city, provides a benchmark against which I evaluate the economic progress of foreign-born Asians and Hispanics. One drawback of this data set is that the U.S. Census does not ascertain whether a respondent is a legal resident of the U.S. While there is no way to precisely estimate the number of undocumented immigrants in the U.S., the Census Bureau estimated that there were between 3,500,000 to 4,000,000 undocumented immigrants living in the U.S. in 1994. Some scholars estimate that the 1990 Census undercounted illegal aliens by approximately 25%, whereas native-born populations were undercounted by approximately 2% (Clark et al 1994). Because the majority of undocumented immigrants are of Hispanic origin (Farley 1996), the Mexican immigrants in this sample may not be representative of the entire population. Despite this weakness, the data clearly provide a wide array of information on household consumption, individual characteristics, and labor force participation, all of which are central to this study. The results of this study will help to clarify contemporary ethnic stratification. In sum, it is the most appropriate sample of the foreign-born living in the U.S.

This sample is restricted to include the non-institutionalized civilian population of working age (16 or older). I further restrict the sample to include only individuals who were employed and reported earnings for 1989. Respondents report industry and status characteristics of their current job. Women and foreign-born non-Hispanic whites are more likely to be excluded from the sample than men and the Asian and Hispanic sub-groups.[24] Given the tendency of women to be unpaid household workers and for the foreign-born non-Hispanic white sample to be older and retired, this finding is not surprising.

I use the metropolitan areas defined by the Geography Division of the Bureau of the Census. I focus on Metropolitan areas, as opposed to the center cities, to include individuals who work in the greater metropolitan area, but who reside outside the core cities.[25] This strategy maximizes the number of immigrants in each of the local labor markets. New York City, Los Angeles and Miami represent Immigrant Metropolis cities for this research because they rank among the top 15 immigrant destinations in 1989[26] as determined by the *Statistical Abstracts* 1991. They also represent the ideal type of a global city because of their international business and trade connections (Ohmae 1990). Denver and Atlanta serve as the complementary Regional Centers for several reasons. Although they rank lower on the list of immigrant destinations, they have substantial minority populations. Furthermore, both are state capitals and major centers of U.S. commerce. Together, these five cities represent different geographic and economic regions across the U.S., ranging from the Northern traditional manufacturing sector, to the Southern newer more service-based economy, to the growing Western communications and manufacturing centers.

RESEARCH DESIGN

This study examines the social and economic attainment of Asian and Hispanic immigrants in five metropolitan cities. The research design I

---

[24]Women are 50.5% of the original sample before the restrictions, but represent 66% of those excluded. Foreign-born non-Hispanic whites are 39% of original sample and 45% of restricted sample.

[25] Consult "Codes, Titles, and Components of Metropolitan Areas" published by the Geography division of the Bureau of Census for the complete listing of metropolitan boundaries.

[26] The 1989 data corresponds most closely to the 1990 Census material.

have chosen permits me to test the model of immigrant attainment presented in Chapter 2. In addition to ethnic heritage, the model includes indicators of human and social capital factors, local labor market characteristics, and social and economic attainment. The principal analytic concern is to understand the association between ethnic background and social and economic attainment and to examine how human capital and local labor market characteristics may affect it.

The discrimination hypothesis posits that ethnic background has a direct effect on social and economic attainment, as well as an indirect effect mediated by human and social capital. A discrimination argument suggests that ethnic heritage has direct effects on earnings and socio-economic status. To the extent that the relationship between ethnic heritage and social and economic attainment is based on ethnic differences in human and social capital and/or local labor market conditions, the possible effects of discrimination are reduced. Discrimination can also affect one's standing on human capital factors and placement in local labor markets. Testing for these effects is outside the scope of this study. I am interested primarily in determining how differences in human and social capital affect the relationship between ethnic heritage and social and economic attainment.

The ethnic heritage measure is a dummy variable for each ethnic group with foreign-born non-Hispanic whites as the reference category. The indicators of human and social capital in this study combine individual and familial resources and deficits. There are four measures of human capital in this model. They are (1) years of schooling, (2) whether the individual completed a college degree, (3) individual labor market experience and its squared term, and (4) language facility. The 1990 Census asks respondents about their highest level of educational attainment (i.e., high school degree), rather than the actual years of schooling. Following Kalmijn (1996), I created a continuous schooling variable (EDUCATION) [27] from the mean number of years required for each grade range: 0 years (kindergarten), 2.5 years (grades 1-4), 6.5 years (grades 5-8), 9 years (grade 9) 10 years (grade 10), 11 years (grade 11), 12 years (grade 12 and high school graduate), 13 years (some college without associate degree in occupational program), 14.5

---

[27] Uppercase letters indicate the actual variable while lowercase letters indicate variable description.

years (associate degree in academic program) 16 years (bachelor's degree) 18 years (master's degree) 22 years (professional and doctorate degrees). Following Dodoo (1997), I also include a dummy variable that measures whether or not the respondent completed a bachelor's degree (BA) in order to capture the potential effects of educational certification.

In order to assess labor market experience, I construct an approximate measure by calculating the respondent's age minus respondent's education minus 6.[28] Because of data limitations, this measure actually assesses the *potential* exposure to the labor market, rather than *actual* participation. Labor market experience and its square (LMEXP, LMEXP2) are the third human capital variables included in this model. I use both variables to capture the curvilinear effect of labor market experience. At the low and high extremes, I expect the coefficient to be negative. In the middle, the returns to labor market experience should be the greatest, and the coefficient should be positive. The final measure of human capital in this model is a self-reported assessment of English language facility included in the Census. On a five point scale, it hierarchically orders individuals in terms of their language ability: those who report that they speak only English at home, those who speak very good English, those who have good speaking ability, those who report poor English speaking ability, (NOT WELL) and those who speak no English at all (NO ENGLISH). The omitted categories in the regression analysis are "only English," "very good English," and "good English" speaking ability.

The social capital variables in this study include measures that assess individual and ethnic constraints and resources. The first variable is a dummy measure of naturalization status, whether an immigrant is a citizen of the U.S. (U.S. CITIZEN). Length of time since immigration is constructed in a series of dummy variables that represent different periods, 1985-1990, 1975-1984, 1965-1974, and pre-1965. The omitted categories in the regression analyses are "1965-1974" and "pre-1965." These periods allow for a comparison of the most recent immigrants to those who have lived in the U.S. longer. Familial constraints/resources are determined with dummy variables that assess whether there is a child under the age of six living in the

---

[28]Age 6 is the generally accepted entrance into the formal schooling system.

household (UNDER6) and whether there is an individual over the age of 65 in the household (OVER65).   Additional control variables include the sex of respondent (FEMALE) and whether the respondent is married (MARRIED).   Male and not currently married are the respective omitted categories.

Finally, my model presumes that local labor market characteristics shape social and economic attainment by placing ethnic workers in areas that either restrict economic advancement or facilitate it. I include several variables that measure specific job characteristics: hours worked per week in 1989 job sector, and occupational status. Hours worked is a continuous measure reported by the Census Bureau (HOURS89). I use the Census division of public, private and self employed to measure job sector (PUBLIC, PRIVATE, SELF).   Private sector is the omitted category in the analysis. I measure occupational prestige with SEI scores derived from the Census occupation codes (SEI).[29]

I include several group and city-specific factors as additional indicators of local labor market conditions. The type of city is indicated by a dummy variable, Immigrant Metropolis (Los Angeles, New York City, and Miami) or Regional Center (Atlanta and Denver), which is the reference category[30]. The level of ethnic concentration of the industry in which the individual works and the sector of employment are also included in this model to measure the effects of the labor market context. Traditionally, an enclave economy has been defined in terms of co-ethnicity of owners and workers, spatial concentration, sector specialization, and functional linkages between many firms run by members of the same ethnic group (Logan et al 1994). I define spatial concentration within metropolitan areas by the

---

[29]Nakao and Treas (1994) update the SEI scores derived from the 1980 Census with data from the 1989 General Social Survey. They also indicate the occupational categories that differ from the 1980 to the 1990 Census so that the scores can be further updated to better fit the 1990 Census.   The only occupational categories that are not sufficiently addressed are military positions, which are excluded in this sample.   This sample includes only non-institutionalized civilians.

[30]Because the Cuban immigrants are concentrated almost exclusively in Miami, the other four cities serve as the reference category for this group.

over-representation of ethnic groups with a particular industry. Sector specialization is measured as an overrepresentation of ethnic workers in a particular industrial category. Following Logan et al (1994) I determine this ratio by cross classifying the foreign-born samples for each city by ethnicity (Chinese, Korean, Filipino, Cuban, or Mexican), followed by the industrial sector in which they work.[31] Then for each ethnic group in each industry, I calculated an over-representation index. I use the percentage of ethnic workers is compared to the percentage of all workers. When this ratio is greater than 1.5, an ethnic concentration in this category exists. For example, if all ethnic workers in an industry = $f1$ and all ethnic workers in the labor force = $f2$, and similarly if all workers (native and foreign-born) in the same industry = $f3$ and *all* workers in the labor force = $f4$, then when the industry concentration as measured by the equation:

$$\frac{f1/f2}{f3/f4} > 1.5$$

an ethnic concentration exists for all ethnic workers in this category. In other words, the percentage of ethnic workers is 1.5 times greater than the percentage of all workers in this industry. This is the only variable that uses the entire city wide population, foreign and native-born in the analysis because to determine ethnic overrepresentation in a particular industry, the entire metropolitan area labor force involved in that industry must be evaluated in order to gauge its relative size.

I use OLS regression analysis to estimate a series of equations. The two dependent variables for the analysis are personal earnings in 1989 dollars (EARN) and occupational prestige scores (SEI) derived from the Census occupation codes. The OLS regressions model a series of equations, beginning with the effect of ethnic background on

---

[31] The twelve industry categories as compiled by the Census are as follows: 1) agriculture, forestry, and fisheries; 2) mining; 3) construction; 4) manufacturing; 5) transportation, communication, and other public utilities; 6) wholesale trade; 7) retail trade; 8) finance, insurance, and real estate; 9) business and repair services; 10) personal services; 11) professional services; 12) public administration.

the social and economic outcomes (SEI) and (EARN). This measures the total effect of ethnic background on attainment. The second set of equations adds human and social capital variables. This analysis measures the effect of ethnic background on attainment net of individual and social resources. The third tier of analysis adds local labor market variables. This model assesses the effect of ethnic background on attainment net of local labor market effects. I also examine the full model, which estimates the effect of ethnic heritage net of human and social capital and local labor market factors on the two measures of attainment. This series of equations permits me to compare the human and social capital model, local labor market model, and full model against the baseline ethnic heritage model. In Chapter 4 I examine the interrelations of the independent variables as they jointly and separately affect stratification between contemporary immigrant groups.

CHAPTER 4:

Analysis

This chapter compares variation in the social and economic attainment of the newest groups of Asian and Hispanic immigrants to that of foreign-born non-Hispanic whites. I present a short descriptive comparison of all six ethnic groups first, followed by the empirical analysis of the immigrant attainment model presented in Chapter 3. These analyses identify the factors that lead to or away from social and economic attainment and describe the general processes that govern it.

Table 4.1 provides descriptive statistics for the six immigrant groups. I note several differences among the five immigrant groups and the comparison population, foreign-born non-Hispanic whites. Cuban immigrants and foreign-born non-Hispanic whites are the oldest groups in the sample and the least likely to have a child under the age of six in the household. Foreign-born non-Hispanic whites report that they have lived in the U.S. the longest of the six groups; 41% arrived before 1965. In contrast, only 3% of Korean immigrants and 4.6% of Filipino immigrants arrived in the same period. All three Asian immigrant groups surpass the comparison group with the proportion holding at least a college degree. Filipino immigrants hold jobs with the highest occupational status of all six groups in the sample. Mexican immigrants, on the other hand, are the youngest, least formally educated, least likely to be naturalized citizens, and the poorest of all the immigrant groups in this sample. They also report the most difficulty with English language facility; 18% report they

Table 4.1: Variable Means for Immigrant Sample

	Chinese	Cuban	Filipino	FBNHW	Korean	Mexican	Average
Age	38.9	44.2	39.0	43.3	38.8	32.2	38.8
Education	13.0	11.8	14.7	13.3	13.8	8.4	11.6
% with College Degree	38.1	17.2	55.3	31.4	38.5	3.0	23.0
Personal Earning ($)	23,668	21,361	25,231	32,176	30,857	13,322	23,082
Family Income ($)	53,831	45,113	62,258	61,992	52,406	34,149	49,619
Labor Market Exp.	19.9	26.4	18.2	24.0	19.0	17.8	21.2
% Speaks Only English	5.3	3.5	8.0	39.0	5.1	3.7	17.0
% English Very Well	32.5	41.0	67.6	36.8	27.1	23.8	34.0
% English Well	32.9	23.8	22.0	17.2	34.5	23.0	22.3
% English Not Well	21.3	20.6	2.2	6.0	29.9	31.6	18.4
% No English	7.9	11.1	0.1	0.9	3.4	17.9	8.4
% Female	46.4	43.5	56.1	41.1	44.0	31.4	40.0
% Married	70.9	66.5	65.0	68.2	73.3	56.4	64.3
% Immigrated 1985-90	21.7	5.8	24.7	12.9	24.4	27.8	19.1
% Immigrated 1975-84	47.3	21.7	43.3	24.2	50.6	39.7	33.6
% Immigrated 1965-74	21.8	41.2	27.4	22.2	21.9	23.8	25.3
% Immigrated before 1965	9.2	31.2	4.6	40.7	3.0	8.7	22.0
% U.S. Citizen	54.2	57.2	53.6	60.3	43.2	20.0	44.7

% in Atlanta	1.7	0.5	0.6	2.6	2.7	0.6	1.5
% in Denver	0.9	0.2	0.6	2.2	2.1	1.0	1.3
% in Los Angeles	46.4	6.5	70.7	32.4	60.0	94.4	55.3
% in Miami	2.5	75.9	1.4	5.9	0.8	0.8	11.5
% in New York	48.5	16.9	26.6	56.8	34.5	3.2	30.3
% Child under 6 at home	7.5	5.5	10.4	4.1	7.4	8.3	6.6
% Over 65 at home	18.2	24.7	20.0	14.8	13.5	6.5	13.7
Hours Worked per week	39.6	39.0	38.4	39.1	41.3	37.2	38.5
% Self Employed	12.0	13.7	4.9	16.8	30.2	5.7	12.1
% in Private Sector	78.6	76.2	81.2	74.1	64.2	90.0	80.0
% in Public Sector	9.3	10.0	13.9	9.0	5.6	4.7	7.9
Number of Workers at home	2.1	2.0	2.2	1.8	1.9	2.1	2.0
SEI	50.3	45.5	52.6	51.9	49.2	33.9	44.9
N	12,277	17,028	10,016	51,184	6,632	49,281	146,418

speak no English at all. The Filipino and Chinese immigrants in the sample have similar levels of economic well-being, although both rank below the standard group in terms of personal earnings. Koreans report the highest level of self- employment in this sample, one that is almost twice that of the reference group. In contrast, Filipino and Mexican immigrants are the least likely to be entrepreneurs. In this sample, the Asian groups earn more than the Hispanic groups, but foreign-born non-Hispanic whites have the highest personal earnings of all six groups.

In terms of residence, the immigrants are not distributed across the five cities evenly. True to their reputations as immigrant destinations, Los Angeles and New York City are the home to many of the immigrants in this sample. However, immigrants are not evenly divided between these two major destinations. The largest numbers of Mexican, Filipino, and Korean immigrants reside in Los Angeles, while foreign-born non-Hispanic whites are more likely to live in New York. Cuban immigrants are concentrated almost exclusively in Miami so that few live elsewhere in the U.S. In contrast, not many immigrants in this sample live in either Denver or Atlanta. In the next section, I examine the immigrant group variation on correlates of integration by reporting the city-to-city differences. I first provide descriptive statistics for foreign-born non-Hispanic whites then describe the target immigrant groups in the sample.

The socio-economic attainment of foreign-born non-Hispanic whites is the benchmark for evaluating the assimilation of the Asian and Hispanic groups in this study. The comparison group is comprised mainly of persons who emigrated from Europe (67.1%). This group also contains smaller numbers of persons from Asia[32] (14.4), Canada (7.3%), Africa (3.0%), and South and Central America[33] (2.9%) who identify as white and non-Hispanic in the 1990 U.S. Census. As shown in Table 4.1, the majority of this group lives in New York City. Overall, individuals in this group possess a high average level of education (13.3 years) and have relatively high status jobs. Foreign-born non-Hispanic whites with the highest level of

---

[32]This category does not include individuals who emigrated from China, Korea, or the Philippines.

[33]This category does not include individuals who emigrated from Mexico.

education reside in Atlanta and Denver, and those with the lowest average years of schooling live in New York City (12.8 years), as shown in Table 4.2. Of all the immigrant groups in this study, the white immigrants have lived in the U.S. the longest on average; 41% arrived in the U.S. before 1965. Perhaps because of the length of time since immigration, a full 39% report speaking only English at home and 60% are naturalized U.S. citizens. Although this group has the highest average personal earnings, differences exist across cities. In Atlanta, foreign-born non-Hispanic whites earn less than both Chinese and Filipino immigrants. In Los Angeles where Asian and Mexican immigrants are concentrated, foreign-born non-Hispanic whites' earnings are the highest of all six groups in this study.

The Chinese immigrants in this study are almost evenly divided between residing Los Angeles and New York City, while the smallest number live in Denver. As shown in Table 4.3, Chinese immigrants report relatively high levels of education on average, ranging from 12.3 years to 14.2 years. In Atlanta, 46% have at least a bachelor's degree. The average years of education for Chinese immigrants is highest in Denver and Atlanta and lowest in New York City, which may reflect that Regional Centers attract a different type of Chinese immigrant than Immigrant Metropolis cities.

The Chinese immigrants in this sample are slightly younger than the comparison group; the average age is 39 for Chinese immigrants as compared to 43 for foreign-born non-Hispanic whites. This group is also more likely to have immigrated recently. In fact, 69% have immigrated since 1975, which may be why almost one third of the sample has low levels of English language facility. This group also ranks lower in terms of household income than the other two Asian groups and the comparison group, which may be due to the timing of their arrival in the U.S. and lower levels of English language facility.

The Cuban immigrants in this study are distinctive because of their almost exclusive residential and occupational concentration in Miami, as shown in Table 4.4. The size of the Cuban immigrant

Table 4.2: Foreign-born non-Hispanic White Variable Means by City

	Los Angeles	Miami	New York	Atlanta	Denver	Average
Age	41.9	43.4	44.5	38.6	40.4	43.3
Education	13.9	13.4	12.8	14.5	14.3	13.3
% with BA	34.1	26.3	29.5	42.1	39.0	31.4
Personal Earnings ($)	33,133	27,039	32,483	30,218	26,394	32,176
Family Income ($)	61,461	51,448	64,084	58,218	48,776	61,992
% Female	41.8	42.5	40.3	45.5	45.3	41.1
% Married	63.4	64.9	71.7	63.9	66.0	68.2
% U.S. Citizen	54.5	54.4	63.9	62.4	67.8	60.3
Child under 6 at home	4.6	4.5	3.6	7.4	6.4	4.1
Over 65 at home	13.3	16.4	16.2	6.8	5.8	14.8
Number of Workers	1.8	1.8	1.9	1.8	1.8	1.8
% Self Employed	19.1	19.7	15.6	13.9	11.7	16.8
% Private Sector	72.1	72.8	75.3	77.2	74.7	74.1

% Public Sector	8.8	7.5	9.1	8.9	13.6	9.0
Hours Worked	39.4	38.9	38.9	40.2	39.6	39.1
% Imm 1985-90	13.0	13.2	12.9	14.6	8.8	12.9
% Imm 1975-84	30.6	30.0	20.1	23.5	18.8	24.2
% Imm 1965-74	19.0	20.7	24.2	22.9	22.1	22.2
% Imm before 1965	37.3	36.1	42.8	39.0	50.3	40.7
% Speaks only	44.7	48.6	32.6	64.4	65.4	39.0
% English very well	37.4	35.9	37.5	26.4	24.8	36.8
% English well	14.2	12.5	20.2	7.1	7.9	17.2
% English not well	3.3	2.4	8.3	2.1	1.9	6.0
%Speaks no English	0.4	0.6	1.3	0.0	0.0	0.9
SEI	54.6	51.9	50.0	56.4	55.7	51.9
Labor Market Exp	22.0	24.0	25.6	18.2	20.1	24.0
N	16,595	3,052	29,073	1,347	1,117	51,184

Table 4.3: Chinese Variable Means by City

	Los Angeles	Miami	New York	Atlanta	Denver	Average
Age	37.9	39.1	40.0	37.7	39.8	38.9
Education	13.7	12.9	12.3	13.7	14.2	13.0
% with BA	41.9	27.9	34.6	45.6	41.5	38.1
Personal Earnings ($)	25,388	22,238	22,148	22,159	23,698	23,668
Family Income ($)	56,799	50,071	51,179	50,357	61,128	53,831
% Female	46.6	48.7	46.4	40.8	45.3	46.4
% Married	67.4	64.7	74.3	75.2	76.4	70.9
% U.S. Citizen	54.8	50.3	54.4	41.7	50.9	54.2
Child Under 6 at home	8.1	5.8	6.9	8.3	11.3	7.5
Over 65 at home	18.8	14.7	18.1	9.2	21.7	18.2
Number of Workers	2.1	2.1	2.1	2.0	2.0	2.1
% Self Employed	14.0	20.2	9.7	14.6	10.4	12.0
% Private Sector	76.3	71.8	8.2	72.3	68.9	78.6

% Public Sector	9.7	8.0	8.7	13.1	20.1	9.3
Hours Worked	38.8	40.9	40.5	40.3	37.9	39.6
% Imm 1985-90	19.7	11.9	23.6	32.5	27.4	21.7
% Imm 1975-84	53.3	56.7	41.2	48.1	42.4	47.3
% Imm 1965-74	19.3	23.4	24.4	13.6	22.6	21.8
% Imm before 1965	7.8	8.0	10.8	5.8	7.5	9.2
% Speaks only English	5.4	34.6	3.7	1.9	10.4	5.3
% English very well	36.5	24.7	29.1	35.9	33.0	32.5
% English well	36.3	26.3	29.8	35.4	34.9	32.9
% English not well	17.9	13.1	25.0	25.7	16.0	21.3
%Speaks no English	3.9	1.3	12.4	1.0	5.7	7.9
SEI	53.3	49.8	47.3	55.1	52.2	50.3
Chinese Industry Conc	1.2	1.7	1.0	1.4	1.5	1.1
Labor Market Exp	18.3	20.3	21.7	18.0	19.6	19.9
N	5,698	312	5,955	206	106	12,277

Table 4.4: Cuban Variable Means by City

	Los Angeles	Miami	New York	Atlanta	Denver	Average
Age	42.7	44.1	45.2	43.5	42.7	44.2
Education	12.3	11.7	12.0	14.3	13.9	11.8
% with BA	19.3	16.1	21.1	39.5	34.4	17.2
Personal Earnings ($)	25,288	19,662	25,882	32,507	20,976	21,361
Family Income ($)	50,024	42,889	52,983	57,429	45,242	45,113
% Female	45.7	43.3	43.4	43.2	51.7	43.5
% Married	67.1	66.5	66.3	80.2	58.6	66.5
% U.S. Citizen	63.8	54.3	67.2	74.1	82.8	57.2
Child Under 6 at home	5.4	5.8	4.7	6.2	13.8	5.5
Over 65 at home	18.4	26.4	19.9	11.1	17.2	24.7
Number of Workers	2.0	2.0	2.0	1.9	1.7	2.0
% Self Employed	13.5	14.3	11.1	16.0	17.2	12.0
% Private Sector	72.4	76.2	78.3	75.3	58.6	78.6

	1,121	12,942	2,892	81	29	17,028
% Public Sector	14.1	9.4	10.6	8.6	24.1	9.3
Hours Worked	38.9	39.0	39.2	39.3	39.0	39.0
% Imm 1985-90	2.8	6.6	3.5	6.2	0.0	5.8
% Imm 1975-84	14.2	23.9	15.1	19.8	10.3	21.7
% Imm 1965-74	53.7	39.0	47.3	13.6	27.6	41.2
% Imm before 1965	29.3	30.5	34.1	60.5	62.1	31.2
% Speaks only English	7.0	2.7	5.5	14.8	10.3	3.5
% English very well	47.4	39.8	43.1	51.9	55.2	41.0
% English well	24.4	23.9	23.5	22.2	17.2	32.9
% English not well	16.6	20.9	21.2	11.1	13.8	21.3
%Speaks no English	4.6	12.7	6.6	0.0	3.4	7.9
SEI	48.2	45.2	45.5	54.4	51.1	45.5
Cuban Industry Conc	1.0	1.5	1.4	1.5	1.9	1.5
Labor Market Exp	24.4	26.4	27.2	23.3	22.8	26.4
N	1,121	12,942	2,892	81	29	17,028

sample in Miami (N= 12,942) is more than four times the Cuban sample that resides in New York City (N= 2,892), the second most popular Cuban destination. At the other extreme, few Cuban immigrants in the sample live in Denver (N= 29) or Atlanta (N= 81). Only a small percentage (5.8%) of Cubans has immigrated since 1985, and those individuals who have, are more likely to live in Miami or Atlanta. Despite the long average length of time Cuban immigrants have spent in the U.S., many report low levels of English language facility. In this sample, 11% of the Cuban immigrants report speaking no English at all. Most Cuban immigrants in this sample are naturalized U.S. citizens and are married with no young children present in the household. In general, the educational, income, and occupational status levels fall well below those of the control group and the three Asian groups. Although most Cuban immigrants choose to live in Miami, they report higher earnings and job status in the other cities. This could be a negative consequence of a highly dense ethnic concentration, a selective migration of low earners to Miami, or a selective migration of high earners to other cities either from Miami or elsewhere.

The majority of Filipino immigrants (71%) in this sample live in Los Angeles as shown in Table 4.5. Los Angeles is clearly the main immigrant metropolis for all of the Asian immigrants in this study, with firmly established Chinatowns, Koreatowns, and a growing Filipino population in this sample. Filipino social and economic attainment varies across cities. In New York, Filipino immigrants have the highest average years of education (15.5), the largest percentage with at least a college degree (69%), and the highest family income ($70,669). In comparison, the Filipino immigrants who reside in Denver have on average 13.4 years of schooling, 40% report at least a college degree, and have a family income of $43,398. In every city except Atlanta, Filipino immigrants have lower personal earnings than foreign-born non-Hispanic whites. Filipino immigrants also have the highest percentage female of all the ethnic groups surveyed, which ranges from 54.4 % in Los Angeles to 75% in Atlanta. On average, more Filipino households than the other groups have children under the age of 6, which varies from a 7.1% low in Atlanta to a high of 23.1% in Denver.

The largest concentration of Korean immigrants in this sample resides in Los Angeles, while the smallest number live in Miami. Economic success for the Korean foreign-born population is highly dependent upon the type of city in which they are employed, as the average household income for Koreans is highest in Los Angeles ($55,620) and lowest in Miami ($35,082), as shown in Table 4.6. As compared to all the other ethnic groups in this sample, Koreans have the highest levels of self-employment (30%), which is almost twice that of the comparison group. Accordingly, their participation in the private and public sectors of the economy is somewhat lower than the other groups' labor force participation.

Although self-employment may be a viable opportunity for the Korean immigrants to use their prior education and skills, their personal income levels are lower than the control group in every city. Social capital deficits may offset their entrepreneurial advantage. Korean immigrants in this sample have been in the U.S. for a relatively short time on average; 75% have immigrated since 1975. Additionally, their level of English language facility is low compared to the other ethnic groups— 33% report low levels of English language facility.

The Mexican immigrants provide a striking contrast to the other immigrants in this study. The majority of Mexican immigrants in this sample reside in Los Angeles (95%). As shown in Table 4.7, Mexican immigrants have lower personal earnings and educational levels than the other immigrant groups in this study in every city. They report earnings less than half the size of the standard group in most cases. In Miami, Mexican immigrants fare better than in any other city; they have higher personal earnings ($14,707), they have jobs with higher occupational status (38.8 SEI), and 8.7% report having a college degree. In New York, half of the Mexican immigrants arrived after 1985 and only 17.8% have become naturalized U.S. citizens. In Los Angeles, Mexican immigrants have the lowest educational credentials; only 2.7% have completed a college degree. Across the cities, Mexican immigrants are young (ranging from 29-33 years), most have young children, and few have older adults in the households. On average 3% report having a college degree and the average level of education is only 8.4 years.

Table 4.5: Filipino Variable Means by City

	Los Angeles	Miami	New York	Atlanta	Denver	Average
Age	38.8	35.3	39.7	37.7	35.6	39.0
Education	14.5	14.4	15.5	15.3	13.4	14.7
% with BA	50.4	55.9	68.8	62.5	40.0	55.3
Personal Earnings ($)	23,192	21,825	30,768	35,552	18,941	25,231
Family Income ($)	59,452	53,200	70,669	61,950	43,398	62,258
% Female	54.4	65.7	59.6	75.0	66.2	56.1
% Married	65.4	64.3	64.3	66.1	66.2	65.0
% U.S. Citizen	55.1	47.6	49.8	57.1	61.5	53.6
Child Under 6 at home	10.7	16.8	9.1	7.1	23.1	10.4
Over 65 at home	20.8	13.3	19.0	8.9	7.7	20.0
Number of Workers	2.2	2.0	2.1	1.8	2.1	2.2
% Self Employed	4.6	0.7	5.7	7.1	4.6	4.9
% Private Sector	80.7	89.5	82.1	80.3	80.0	81.2

% Public Sector	14.7	9.8	12.2	12.5	15.4	13.9
Hours Worked	38.4	36.5	38.3	39.8	39.7	38.4
% Imm 1985-90	23.4	24.4	27.9	19.6	32.3	24.7
% Imm 1975-84	45.7	51.7	36.8	30.4	40.0	43.3
% Imm 1965-74	25.9	18.9	31.8	45.7	23.1	27.4
% Imm before 1965	4.9	4.9	3.6	14.3	4.6	4.6
% Speaks only English	7.5	14.7	8.3	28.6	21.5	8.0
% English very well	67.5	66.4	68.5	66.1	58.5	67.6
% English well	22.7	17.5	21.0	5.4	20.0	22.0
% English not well	2.2	1.4	2.2	0.0	0.0	2.2
%Speaks no English	0.2	0.0	0.1	0.0	0.0	0.1
SEI	50.5	56.0	57.8	60.3	45.8	52.6
Filipino Industry Conc	1.5	2.1	1.7	1.6	1.3	1.6
Labor Market Exp	18.4	14.8	18.2	16.4	16.3	18.2
N	7,086	143	2,666	56	65	10,016

Table 4.6: Korean Variable Means by City

	Los Angeles	Miami	New York	Atlanta	Denver	Average
Age	38.8	36.8	39.0	38.6	37.1	38.8
Education	13.8	13.3	14.0	13.5	13.1	13.8
% with BA	37.5	28.3	41.7	30.1	28.9	38.5
Personal Earnings ($)	26,413	15,923	24,878	21,724	17,984	30,857
Family Income ($)	55,621	35,082	52,264	44,393	44,325	52,406
% Female	43.8	54.7	43.3	42.6	58.5	44.0
% Married	73.3	75.5	73.2	74.4	73.9	73.3
% U.S. Citizen	44.0	43.3	40.9	45.5	55.6	43.2
Child Under 6 at home	7.6	7.5	6.6	9.1	14.1	7.4
Over 65 at home	13.4	7.5	14.6	3.4	10.6	13.5
Number of Workers	2.0	1.7	1.9	2.1	2.0	1.9
% Self Employed	32.5	32.1	26.9	30.7	16.2	30.2
% Private Sector	61.8	60.4	68.5	61.4	67.6	64.2

% Public Sector	5.6	7.5	4.7	8.0	16.2	5.6
Hours Worked	41.0	37.2	42.6	42.1	41.6	41.3
% Imm 1985-90	22.3	34.0	27.9	27.3	20.4	24.4
% Imm 1975-84	52.4	35.8	47.5	48.9	55.6	50.6
% Imm 1965-74	22.3	18.9	21.5	21.0	21.1	21.9
% Imm before 1965	2.9	11.3	3.1	2.8	2.8	3.0
% Speaks only English	4.4	26.4	5.0	9.6	10.6	5.1
% English very well	27.6	30.2	26.1	28.4	31.0	27.1
% English well	34.9	24.5	34.3	29.0	35.9	34.5
% English not well	30.0	15.1	31.3	30.1	20.4	29.9
%Speaks no English	3.5	3.8	3.4	2.8	2.1	3.4
SEI	49.2	49.3	50.0	43.5	43.1	49.2
Korean Industry Conc	1.3	1.9	1.1	1.8	1.7	1.3
Labor Market Exp	19.1	17.5	19.0	19.1	18.0	19.0
N	3,972	53	2,289	176	142	6,632

Table 4.7: Mexican Variable Means by City

	Los Angeles	Miami	New York	Atlanta	Denver	Average
Age	32.3	32.8	30.3	29.3	32.8	32.2
Education	8.4	9.3	9.5	9.3	8.1	8.4
% with BA	2.7	8.7	8.5	8.4	3.5	3.0
Personal Earnings ($)	13,330	14,707	13,418	13,239	11,706	23,082
Family Income ($)	34,307	30,650	35,403	25,039	25,064	49,619
% Female	31.7	32.0	26.0	20.0	29.7	31.4
% Married	56.6	57.5	49.7	52.6	59.4	56.4
% U.S. Citizen	20.0	21.2	17.8	21.1	33.8	20.0
Child Under 6 at home	8.5	7.9	4.6	5.5	8.2	8.3
Over 65 at home	6.6	5.4	4.4	1.6	4.9	6.5
Number of Workers	2.1	1.8	2.1	1.8	1.9	2.1
% Self Employed	5.7	9.0	4.5	6.5	4.1	5.7
% Private Sector	9.0	85.9	92.5	90.6	90.3	90.0

% Public Sector	4.7	5.6	2.9	3.0	5.1	4.8
Hours Worked	37.2	36.5	37.0	38.3	39.2	37.1
% Imm 1985-90	27.8	21.8	45.8	50.0	35.8	27.0
% Imm 1975-84	39.7	44.5	38.0	34.4	40.4	40.0
% Imm 1965-74	23.8	25.6	12.7	10.4	14.3	24.4
% Imm before 1965	8.7	8.0	3.6	5.3	9.5	8.8
% Speaks only English	3.7	4.9	4.5	5.9	4.3	3.6
% English very well	23.8	24.1	24.0	24.5	25.6	23.8
% English well	23.0	26.4	18.5	18.5	18.9	23.2
% English not well	31.6	32.6	37.0	32.5	27.4	31.6
%Speaks no English	31.6	12.0	15.9	18.5	23.8	17.9
SEI	33.9	33.5	34.8	34.1	38.8	33.9
Mexican Industry Conc	1.5	1.6	3.2	1.8	1.5	1.5
Labor Market Exp	17.8	18.7	14.0	14.8	17.5	17.9
N	**49,281**	**485**	**308**	**1577**	**391**	**46,582**

DISCUSSION

To sum, immigrant social and economic attainment varies across ethnic groups and, to a lesser extent, across cities. The most significant differences are those between ethnic groups. In comparison to all the other immigrant groups, foreign-born non- Hispanic whites report the highest income levels, and Filipino immigrants have the highest average educational credentials and occupational status. All three Asian groups rank lower than foreign-born non-Hispanic whites in terms of personal earnings, however, they earn more than both Hispanic immigrant groups in this study. Koreans, overall, have fallen into a strong entrepreneurial niche, using prior investments in human capital to start small businesses. In contrast, Filipino immigrants have embarked upon a different trajectory. Many of the jobs they find are in the public sector with relatively high SEI scores and lower pay. In general, Asians are more likely to have both children and older family members in their households than the control group, which may help offset some of the strain of a two- worker family. Overall, the state of Asian immigrants is quite positive.

In contrast to the three Asian groups, the Hispanic immigrants have more varied experiences. Cuban immigrants live primarily in Miami. The Cubans in this sample are mainly older immigrants who report living in the U.S. nearly as long as the comparison group. Despite these benefits, their economic attainment is not as positive as it is for other groups in this study. They report lower personal and family incomes than all the other groups except Mexican immigrants. In comparison, the Mexican immigrants in this sample settled largely in Los Angeles, which is not surprising given that city's proximity to the Mexican border. This group scores the lowest in terms of socioeconomic attainment— on average, they have the lowest education, income, and occupational status levels in the study. Furthermore, Mexican immigrants report the lowest levels of English language facility. Most are recent immigrants and fewer than 25% have become naturalized U.S. citizens.

Although the descriptive data show small differences between Immigrant Metropolis cities and Regional Centers, the most interesting findings are the contrasts between the different ethnic groups. The lack of strong city differences may be due in part to the small numbers of immigrants in this sample who live in the Regional Centers, which does not permit strong comparisons to be made. Regardless of city type, the number of workers in each household is high. The percent self-employed does not vary dramatically across city type, nor does the average household income, or hours worked per week. Only when ethnic groups are compared do differences become evident. In general, immigrants come to the U.S. to find a better life and economic success. To achieve that, they tend to work long hours, rely on all the members of a household to contribute in both paid and non-paid employment, take financial risks to start a small business, and sometimes work in jobs that native-born Americans reject.

To this point, I have described the economic and social attainment of contemporary Asian and Hispanic immigrants and have compared them to foreign-born non-Hispanic whites. This comparison identifies ethnic background as an important variable to consider in immigrant social and economic attainment. I present statistical analysis in the next section which evaluates the importance of human and social capital and local labor market processes in assessing ethnic differences in the socio-economic attainments of foreign-born Americans.

QUANTITATIVE ANALYSIS

In the analyses that follow, I use OLS regression to estimate competing models of economic and social attainment. For each ethnic group, I examine the effects that ethnic background, human and social capital factors, and local labor market indicators have on personal earnings and occupational status attainment. Foreign-born non-Hispanic whites are the comparison group for each set of analyses.

The equations in Tables 4.8-4.19 model the earnings and occupational status attainment processes for the six immigrant groups. For each table, Model 1 describes the basic relationship between ethnic heritage and earnings and occupational attainments. The R^2 value shows how much of the total variation in the dependent variables is associated with differences in ethnic heritage. Model 2 reveals how much variation in earnings and occupational status is associated with human and social capital factors. Change in the ethnic background

Table 4.8: OLS Regression of Personal Earnings for Foreign-born non-Hispanic Whites

	MODEL 1		MODEL 2		MODEL 3		MODEL 4	
	Coef.	S.E.	Coef.	S.E.	Coef	S.E.	Coef.	S.E.
Intercept	18,194.00	83.85	3,321.96	373.74	-23,487.00	254.85	-22,931.00	426.52
Ethnic Background								
FBNHW	13,983.00	141.82	6,180.52	142.13	6,778.55	139.33	4,289.94	143.08
Human/Social Capital								
Education			1,034.37	19.99			630.05	19.31
BA			11,276.00	194.23			5,075.47	191.96
English Not Well			-3,569.27	177.15			-1,955.27	166.86
No English			-2,893.54	249.03			621.96	233.91
U.S. Citizen			1,636.42	143.49			927.99	135.26
Imm 85-90			-8,024.55	243.30			-6,539.30	229.23
Imm 75-84			-4,837.10	198.46			-4,582.89	186.65
Imm 65-74			-2,041.28	189.28			-2,139.97	177.42
Child under 6			714.09	266.83			848.29	249.81

	Model 1		Model 2		Model 3		Model 4	
	Coef.	SE	Coef.	SE	Coef.	SE	Coef.	SE
Over 65 at home			-2,712.54	190.00			-1,949.54	177.95
Labor Mkt Exp			851.21	15.44			598.32	14.63
Labor Mkt Exp^2			-13.33	0.28			-8.82	0.27
Female			-10,916.00	132.28			-7,793.80	126.18
Married			3,260.52	141.04			2,335.11	132.27
Labor Market Context								
Hours Worked					489.47	4.11	399.03	4.07
Public Sector					-1,985.21	222.68	-3,658.19	215.53
Self Employed					6,993.06	183.65	4,387.69	178.46
New York City					4,045.35	195.19	4,136.44	189.01
Los Angeles					1,982.73	174.46	3,444.47	171.84
SEI					497.20	3.17	343.11	3.77
R^2	0.06		0.26		0.30		0.35	
N	146,418							

Table 4.9: OLS Regression of Occupational Status Attainment for Foreign-born non-Hispanic Whites

	MODEL 1		MODEL 2		MODEL 3		MODEL 4	
	Coef.	S.E.	Coef.	S.E.	Coef.	S.E.	Coef.	S.E.
Intercept	41.13	0.06	30.17	0.24	37.23	0.19	29.93	0.29
Ethnic Background								
FBNHW	10.77	0.10	2.99	0.09	9.12	0.11	3.28	0.10
Human/Social Capital								
Education			1.06	0.01			0.99	0.01
BA			15.72	0.13			15.52	0.13
English Not Well			-4.92	0.12			-4.79	0.12
No English			-4.54	0.16			-4.40	0.16
U.S. Citizen			2.03	0.09			1.84	0.09
Imm 85-90			-4.32	0.16			-3.78	0.16
Imm 75-84			-3.10	0.13			-2.84	0.13
Imm 65-74			-1.45	0.12			-1.35	0.12
Child under 6			0.60	0.17			0.63	0.17

	Model 1		Model 2		Model 3	
Over 65 at home	-0.24	0.12			-0.21	0.12
Labor Mkt Exp	0.08	0.01			0.03	0.01
Labor Mkt Exp^2	0.00	0.00			0.00	0.00
Female	-2.24	0.09			-1.90	0.09
Married	0.87	0.09			0.76	0.09
Labor Market/Context						
Hours Worked			0.14	0.00	0.06	0.00
Public Sector			12.81	0.18	5.26	0.15
Self Employed			6.25	0.15	3.46	0.12
New York			-1.52	0.16	-1.92	0.13
Los Angeles			-4.16	0.14	-1.65	0.12
R^2	0.42		0.12		0.43	
N	146,418					

coefficient as compared to Model 1 can be attributed to ethnic differences in human and social capital. Similarly, Model 3 estimates the effects of local labor market factors. Change in the ethnic background coefficient as compared to Model 1 is due to ethnic differences in local labor market factors. Model 4 includes all human and social capital factors as well as the local labor market indicators. The R^2 value shows how much total variation is associated with the three levels of factors. These successive models explain why ethnic group membership makes a difference in social and economic attainment. I begin by comparing the attainments of foreign-born non-Hispanic whites with all the non-white ethnics in the sample. After that, I present detailed pair-wise analyses of each non-white ethnic group with the comparison group.

Foreign-born Non-Hispanic Whites

I report the personal earnings parameter estimates for foreign-born non-Hispanic whites and all non-white groups in Table 4.8. In Model 1, the zero-order relationship between ethnic background and earnings for this sample is $13,983. This suggests that without controlling for other group differences, white immigrants earn significantly more than their non-white counterparts. However, very little of the variation in income attainment is associated with ethnic heritage alone as indicated by small R^2. Yet, ethnic heritage has a statistically significant and sizeable effect on earnings.

When I estimate the effect of the human and social capital variables in Model 2, FBNHW reduces to $6,180. Fifty-six percent of the covariation of FBNHW and personal earnings is due to ethnic differences in human and social capital. Years of schooling, having a college degree, labor market experience, being a naturalized citizen, being married, or having a young child in the household are all positive and significant. Low levels of English language facility, arriving in the U.S. after 1975, being female, or having an older household member are negative and significant. Because foreign-born non-Hispanic whites are more likely than the non-white immigrants in this sample to have immigrated to the U.S. earlier, to be a naturalized U.S. citizen, and to have higher levels of English language facility, they maintain an earnings advantage. These findings are consistent with the human and social capital argument, which makes the claim that investments in skills are associated with greater monetary returns, while competing demands on personal times have negative effects. Although members of some non-white immigrant groups have better human capital investments than foreign-born non- Hispanic whites, a substantial component of the ethnic difference in earnings is due to the white ethnic group members' advantage on these factors. Furthermore, white ethnic workers would have even greater net advantages if their human and social capital investments were consistently superior to the non-white immigrants in this sample.

In Model 3, I estimate the effects of the local labor market conditions and ethnic heritage. The local labor market variables decrease the size of the ethnicity parameter by 52% ($7,204) from Model 1. Yet, even after accounting for the location and sectors where immigrants work, FBNHW has a positive and significant effect on earnings. Differences in local labor market factors, such as living in New York City, advantage white ethnics in this sample. Model 4 includes the human and social capital factors as well as the local labor market indicators. In this model, the ethnicity coefficient is $4,290, which is a 69% reduction over Model 1. The R^2 in Model 4 improves to 0.35, which suggests the importance of both human and social capital factors and local labor market context. In addition, the change in the size of FBNHW indicates that both sets of factors mediate the relationship between ethnic heritage and personal earnings. Despite the substantial reduction in FBNHW, there is still a difference of close to $4,300 with non-white immigrants with respect to personal earnings. Foreign-born non-Hispanic whites maintain higher earnings than the five non-white groups, even after controlling for ethnic differences in the independent variables. The residual earnings difference may be due to the effects of other unmeasured effects including discrimination.

The next four equations examine the effects of the independent variables on SEI as shown in Table 4.9. In Model 1, FBNHW is positive and significant. Foreign-born non-Hispanic whites have substantially higher status jobs than do the other ethnics in this sample. In this model, the occupational status difference between the white and non-white immigrants is 11 SEI points. When I add the human and social capital variables in Model 2, FBNHW decreases in size to 2.99. This means that 72% of the covariation of FBNHW and SEI is due to ethnic differences in human and social capital. The signs of the human capital variables in Model 2 are similar to those in the personal earnings model. Being female, having poor English speaking skills, and immigrating after 1975 are negative, while years of education and having a college degree are positive. Equating the groups on human and social capital factors would substantially reduce the gap in job status, although white ethnics would maintain a slight edge over the non-white immigrants in this study.

The third model estimates the effect the city level regressors on occupational attainment. The size of the ethnicity coefficient decreases by 15% from Model 1 to Model 3. Ethnic differences on local labor market factors advantage white ethnics. Living in Los Angeles or in New York City has a negative and significant effect on occupational status. However, both public sector employment and self-employment have positive and significant effects on status, which may offset other deficits for this group.

In the full model, FBNHW becomes 70% smaller as compared to Model 1. The occupational status gap between foreign-born non-Hispanic whites and the non-white immigrant groups would be narrowed considerably if ethnic differences in human and social capital and local labor market conditions were eliminated. Yet, foreign-born non-Hispanic whites have higher occupational status than do the other immigrant groups even after controlling for these differences. The next section compares the regressions for each of the Asian and Hispanic ethnic groups to foreign-born non-Hispanic whites

Chinese Immigrants

The first model in Table 4.10 examines the sole effect of Chinese ethnic heritage on personal earnings as compared to foreign-born non-Hispanic whites. The ethnic background coefficient is negative and significant, indicating that Chinese immigrants earn about $8,500 less than the comparison group. Once I estimate the effects of the human and social capital variables in Model 2, CHINESE decreases by 52% to approximately $4,100. The education variables, labor market experience, and current married status are all positive and significant. Recent immigration to the U.S., low levels of English language facility, having an older household member, or being female have negative and significant effects. Given that Chinese immigrants are more likely than foreign-born non-Hispanic whites to be recent U.S.

arrivals or to have some difficulty with speaking English, their personal earnings are lower. Yet, even after controlling for differences in education and resources, Chinese ethnics would earn less than the standard group, as indicated by the $4,100 ethnic earnings residual. When I estimate the effect of the city level variables in Model 3, Chinese decreases 46% as compared to Model 1. This suggests that the location where immigrants work explains some of covariation between ethnic background on personal earnings. Holding these variables constant, the gap in earnings between Chinese and foreign-born non-Hispanic white workers would be closed substantially. Self-employment or working in either Immigrant Metropolis city is positive and significant. However, given the greater likelihood for Chinese immigrants to work in the public sector or in a Chinese concentrated concentrated industry, their earnings are lower than the earnings of foreign-born non-Hispanic white workers. The Chinese disadvantage in personal earnings is due, in part, to local labor market characteristics, but also is offset somewhat by advantages in human and social capital variables.

In the full model, CHINESE is no longer statistically significant. Holding labor market context and human and social capital constant, there would be no statistically significant difference in earnings between Chinese and foreign-born non-Hispanic white workers. There remains a $1,000 deficit in earnings; however, it falls within the normal income distribution. These analyses show that almost all of the gap in earnings between Chinese immigrants and foreign-born non-Hispanic whites is due to ethnic differences in human capital and local labor market characteristics.

In Table 4.11, the effect of CHINESE on SEI is negative and significant in Model 1. Chinese immigrants have slightly lower occupational status than foreign-born non-Hispanic whites. With the inclusion of the human and social capital variables in Model 2, Chinese has a small positive and significant effect on SEI. When human and social capital factors are taken into account, the status difference between Chinese workers and the comparison group is minimized. Both measures of education, being a naturalized U.S. citizen, or being currently married have positive and significant effects on SEI. English language facility, recent immigration, being female,

Table 4.10: OLS Regression of Personal Earnings for Chinese Immigrants

	MODEL 1		MODEL 2		MODEL 3		MODEL 4	
	Coef.	S.E.	Coef.	S.E.	Coef.	S.E.	Coef.	S.E.
Intercept	32,176.00	144.41	2,595.60	801.80	-28,305.00	541.71	-32,616.00	886.70
Ethnic Background								
CHINESE	-8,508.86	328.32	-4,094.46	320.34	-4,622.80	674.27	-1,049.83	660.87
Human/Social Capital								
Education			1,476.70	46.20			908.79	44.54
BA			10,124.00	366.35			4,055.42	352.88
English Not Well			-6,040.77	447.99			-3,560.38	421.35
No English			-3,993.60	843.87			-2,488.74	791.69
U.S. Citizen			331.91	278.58			91.82	260.61
Imm 85-90			-7,734.87	468.97			-5,714.61	438.25
Imm 75-84			-3,642.45	357.01			-3,365.86	334.41
Imm 65-74			-604.83	338.73			-849.23	316.38
Child under 6			-890.95	580.89			52.60	542.40

	Model 1		Model 2		Model 3		Model 4	
	b	SE	b	SE	b	SE	b	SE
Over 65 at home			-3,916.08	358.98			-2,690.67	335.22
Labor Mkt Exp			1,031.39	29.45			723.80	27.83
Labor Mkt Exp^2			-14.97	0.52			-9.39	0.50
Female			-15,713.00	246.85			-10,753.00	237.80
Married			4,535.68	278.11			3,475.50	260.18
Labor Market Context								
Hours Worked					661.48	7.88	538.06	7.88
Public Sector					-4,101.87	401.07	-5,527.51	386.30
Self Employed					7,531.39	313.77	4,101.46	305.46
New York City					6,506.01	394.38	5,535.45	380.10
Los Angeles					4,801.59	410.87	4,674.23	393.69
Chinese Industry					-2,728.51	532.46	-3,133.43	511.66
SEI					548.43	5.56	384.08	6.62
R^2	0.01		0.22		0.26		0.32	
N	63,461							

Table 4.11: OLS Regression of Occupational Status Attainment for Chinese Immigrants

	MODEL 1		MODEL 2		MODEL 3		MODEL 4	
	Coef.	S.E.	Coef.	S.E.	Coef.	S.E.	Coef.	S.E.
Intercept	51.90	0.09	27.91	0.45	45.64	0.34	26.01	0.52
Ethnic Background								
CHINESE	-1.60	0.21	0.70	0.18	4.08	0.48	2.75	0.40
Human/Social Capital								
Education			1.63	0.03			1.57	0.03
BA			12.52	0.21			12.23	0.21
English Not Well			-6.90	0.25			-6.45	0.25
No English			-7.72	0.48			-7.39	0.47
U.S. Citizen			0.56	0.16			0.56	0.16
Imm 85-90			-3.24	0.26			-2.89	0.26
Imm 75-84			-2.07	0.20			-2.16	0.20
Imm 65-74			-1.19	0.19			-1.10	0.19
Child under 6			1.05	0.33			1.21	0.32

	(1)		(2)		(3)	
Over 65 at home	-1.19	0.20			-1.06	0.20
Labor Mkt Exp	0.00	0.02			-0.06	0.02
Labor Mkt Exp^2	0.00	0.00			0.00	0.00
Female	-2.85	0.14			-2.37	0.14
Married	0.90	0.16			0.90	0.16
Labor Market Context						
Hours Worked			0.17	0.01	0.08	0.00
Public Sector			10.76	0.28	4.80	0.23
Self Employed			4.04	0.22	2.27	0.18
New York City			-4.06	0.28	-1.66	0.23
Los Angeles			0.82	0.29	0.57	0.24
Chinese Industry			-5.29	0.38	-2.07	0.31
R^2	0.38		0.06		0.39	
N	0.00					
	63,461					

or having younger or older members in the household have negative and significant effects on SEI. Chinese immigrants have better investments in human capital that offset social capital deficits in terms of occupational status. In Model 3, I estimate the effect of the local labor market variables on occupational status. In this model, CHINESE is positive and 536% larger than it was in Model 1. Controlling for differences in the local labor markets would decrease the gap in occupational status between foreign-born non-Hispanic whites and Chinese immigrants. Living in New York City or working in a Chinese concentrated industry have negative and significant effects on SEI. Given the likelihood of Chinese immigrants to work longer hours and to work in the public sector there is a positive and significant effect on their SEI scores. In Model 4, Chinese ethnicity variable is positive and significant. These data suggest that if Chinese immigrants and foreign-born non-Hispanic whites had similar levels of human capital, received similar returns to human capital investments, and were equated on local labor market characteristics, Chinese immigrants would have advantageous occupational status. Human capital and local labor market arguments explain the status gap that advantages foreign-born non-Hispanic whites in this sample.

Cuban Immigrants

Model 1 in Table 4.12 shows that CUBAN has a negative and significant effect on personal earnings. Cuban immigrants earn substantially ($10,800) less than foreign-born non-Hispanic whites. However, the small R^2 in this model indicates the low explanatory power of ethnic heritage alone. In Model 2, I estimate the effects of human and social capital variables on personal earnings. In this model, CUBAN decreases by 46% but remains negative and significant. The statistically significant effects of all variables except U.S. CITIZEN are consistent with support for human and social capital arguments. Immigrating after 1975, English language facility, being female, having a young child, or having an older household member are negative and significant. Education, labor market experience, or being currently married are positive and significant. If Cubans were equated with the standard group on human capital factors, the difference in their earnings would be almost cut in half. In Model 3, the Cuban ethnic heritage coefficient remains negative and significant. Accounting for differences in the local labor market explains 63% of the difference in personal earnings between Cuban workers and foreign-born non-Hispanic white workers. Working in the public sector or living in Miami have negative and significant effects on personal earnings, while self-employment is positive and significant. Given the greater likelihood of Cuban immigrants to reside in Miami as compared to foreign-born non-Hispanic whites, this has a disproportionate negative effect on their earnings.

CUBAN has a negative and significant effect on earnings in the full model. The size of the earnings gap between foreign-born non-Hispanic whites and Cubans in this model is approximately $2,700. This residual ethnic effect could be due to unmeasured factors, including racial and ethnic discrimination. Between Models 1 and 4, the size of the Cuban ethnicity coefficient decreases 75%. Equating Cuban immigrants and the comparison group with respect to human capital and local labor market variables would close the earnings gap by roughly $8,000. The R^2 in the full model improves to 0.32, which indicates the importance of both human and social capital factors and local labor market indicators as sources of variation in personal earnings.

The effect of CUBAN on SEI in Model 1 is negative and significant in Table 4.13. The gap in occupational status in this model is more than 6 SEI points. Accounting for differences in the human and social capital variables in Model 2 explains a substantial amount of the effect of Cuban ethnicity on SEI attainment. Eighty-seven percent of the covariation between ethnic background and SEI can be accounted for by ethnic differences in human and social capital. The status gap in this model is less than 1 SEI point.

In Model 3, I estimate the effect of the labor market variables and ethnic heritage on occupational status attainment. In this model, CUBAN has a positive and significant effect. Controlling for where Cuban immigrants work explains some of the difference in occupational status. Given the greater likelihood of Cuban workers as compared to foreign-born non-Hispanic whites to work in Cuban concentrated industries, their occupational status suffers. Cubans would have higher SEI scores if they were placed in more

Table 4.12: OLS Regression of Personal Earnings for Cuban Immigrants

	MODEL 1		MODEL 2		MODEL 3		MODEL 4	
	Coef.	S.E.	Coef.	S.E.	Coef.	S.E.	Coef.	S.E.
Intercept	32,176.00	139.67	5,308.05	746.79	-21,784.00	395.70	-25,813.00	767.84
Ethnic Background								
CUBAN	-10,802.00	279.32	-5,858.37	273.77	-4,003.51	553.92	-2,729.64	537.16
Human/Social Capital								
Education			1,418.35	44.14			819.94	42.37
BA			10,138.00	355.46			4,378.72	341.20
English Not Well			-5,680.22	409.33			-2,919.93	383.93
No English			-3,513.82	664.73			-739.00	623.87
U.S. Citizen			167.17	260.31			-154.87	243.24
Imm 85-90			-8,022.71	454.80			-5,658.13	424.90
Imm 75-84			-4,424.76	335.22			-3,728.36	313.31
Imm 65-74			-1,665.11	295.16			-1,678.43	275.55
Child under 6			-1,240.30	560.05			-95.60	522.78

	b	SE	b	SE	b	SE	b	SE
Over 65 at home			-4,009.59	325.80			-2,407.96	304.34
Labor Mkt Exp			921.98	27.51			676.35	25.93
Labor Mkt Exp^2			-13.56	0.48			-8.84	0.46
Female			-15,682.00	231.60			-10,667.00	223.38
Married			4,726.33	252.44			3,637.43	235.71
Labor Market Context								
Hours Worked					669.24	7.61	544.60	7.62
Public Sector					-3,564.75	373.19	-5,063.83	360.68
Self Employed					7,144.22	291.67	3,722.09	284.42
Miami					-5,547.61	356.25	-4,610.54	343.27
Cuban Industry					506.02	319.29	88.54	308.98
SEI					524.83	5.41	381.36	6.32
R^2	0.02		0.22		0.26		0.32	
N	68,249							

Table 4.13: OLS Regression of Occupational Status Attainment for Cuban Immigrants

	MODEL 1		MODEL 2		MODEL 3		MODEL 4	
	Coef.	S.E.	Coef.	S.E.	Coef	S.E.	Coef.	S.E.
Intercept	51.90	0.09	28.64	0.43	42.46	0.23	25.07	0.46
Ethnic Background								
CUBAN	-6.37	0.18	-0.81	0.16	1.31	0.39	1.72	0.33
Human/Social Capital								
Education			1.59	0.03			1.55	0.03
BA			12.24	0.20			11.77	0.20
English Not Well			-5.92	0.23			-5.54	0.23
No English			-4.62	0.38			-3.98	0.38
U.S. Citizen			1.05	0.15			0.87	0.15
Imm 85-90			-3.58	0.26			-3.24	0.26
Imm 75-84			-2.41	0.19			-2.31	0.19
Imm 65-74			-1.58	0.17			-1.54	0.17
Child under 6			1.17	0.32			1.41	0.32

Over 65 at home	-0.91	0.19		-0.75	0.18
Labor Mkt Exp	-0.03	0.02		-0.08	0.02
Labor Mkt Exp^2	0.00	0.00		0.00	0.00
Female	-2.69	0.13		-1.99	0.14
Married	1.29	0.14		1.16	0.14
Labor Market Context					
Hours Worked			0.20	0.01	0.10	0.00
Public Sector			10.02	0.26	4.21	0.22
Self Employed			4.14	0.21	2.53	0.17
Miami			0.02	0.25	0.84	0.21
Cuban Industry			-5.37	0.22	-2.35	0.19
R^2	0.02	0.36	0.07	0.38
N	68,249			

advantageous labor market positions as compared to foreign-born non-Hispanic white workers.

When I estimate the full model, CUBAN remains positive and significant. Differences in individual resources and the location or sector where Cuban immigrants work, in this case the greater likelihood to work in a Cuban concentrated industry or to have lower investments in human capital, explains how ethnic background influences occupational status. These data indicate that if differences in human and social capital and local labor market conditions between Cuban immigrants and foreign-born non-Hispanic whites were eliminated, the gap in occupational status would reverse.

Filipino Immigrants

Model 1 in Table 4.14 examines the sole effect of the Filipino ethnic heritage on income attainment. As compared to the standard group, Filipino has a negative and significant effect on personal earnings. The R^2 in this model is small, which suggests that ethnic background alone is associated with very little of the total variance in personal earnings. With the addition of the individual background variables in Model 2, the size of the Filipino coefficient decreases slightly to -$6,067. Only 13% of the covariation between FILIPINO and personal earnings is accounted for by ethnic differences in human and social capital. The human capital advantages that Filipino immigrants have are offset by a greater proportion female, slightly lower marriage rates, and less labor market experience.

The effect of the city level regressors in Model 3 decreases the size of FILIPINO by 6.5% as compared to Model 1. Accounting for the location of work for Filipino immigrants explains only a small part of the gap in earning between the two groups. Living in New York City or Los Angeles, being self-employed, and occupational status all have positive and significant effects on personal earnings. Because Filipino workers are more likely than the comparison group to live in Los Angeles, but less likely to be self-employed, this explains the slight decrease in the status gap between the two groups. In Model 4, the size of FILIPINO increases 10.5% and still has a negative effect on economic attainment. If Filipino immigrants and the comparison group were equated in terms of human and social capital and local labor market conditions, the earnings difference between the two groups would actually increase. Human capital and social capital factors and local labor market conditions separately explain only a small portion of the earnings gap between Filipino immigrants and foreign-born non-Hispanic whites. When both sets of factors are included in the full model, the Filipino earnings disadvantage increases. This suggests that Filipino workers are disadvantaged by other factors, possibly including discrimination, which are not measured in this study. Differences in earnings between Filipino immigrants and the comparison group cannot be addressed solely by examining differences in human and social capital and local labor market conditions.

The Filipino SEI equations in Table 4.15 diverge from the income attainment pattern. The effect of Filipino background on SEI is positive and significant in Model 1. Filipino workers have jobs with slightly higher status (less than 1 SEI point) than foreign-born non-Hispanic white workers. The size of FILIPINO increases by a factor of 6, and its direction is reversed in Model 2. When ethnic differences on human and social capital factors are taken into account, the slight edge Filipino workers have with respect to SEI is eliminated and a large foreign-born non-Hispanic white advantage is revealed. The small zero-order Filipino advantage is due to the slightly superior human capital factors they possess. Being female, having an older household member, recently immigrating, and low levels of language facility are all negative and significant in this model. Since Filipino immigrants are more likely than the comparison group to have these social capital deficits, this adversely affects their SEI scores. Education, labor market experience, and being a naturalized citizen have positive and significant effects on personal earnings. These human capital advantages offset social capital deficits for Filipino workers.

In Model 3, Filipino decreases dramatically, from 0.67 in Model 1 to –15.5. This suggests that local labor market conditions mediate the relationship between ethnic background and job status, and they work to the advantage of Filipino workers. Living in New York City is negative and significant, but living in Los Angeles does not have a significant effect on SEI. Working in a Filipino concentrated industry, working in the public sector, or being self-employed also have positive and significant effects on SEI. Because Filipino workers are more

Table 4.14: OLS Regression of Personal Earnings for Filipino Immigrants

	MODEL 1		MODEL 2		MODEL 3		MODEL 4	
	Coef.	S.E.	Coef.	S.E.	Coef.	S.E.	Coef.	S.E.
Intercept	32,176.00	143.06	986.23	833.67	-29,463.00	552.17	-35,077.00	911.26
Ethnic Background								
FILIPINO	-6,945.63	353.64	-6,066.95	342.84	-6,492.31	808.08	-7,673.34	782.71
Human/Social Capital								
Education			1,715.98	50.04			1,042.41	48.03
BA			8,474.59	372.11			2,424.06	354.74
English Not Well			-4,880.44	548.67			-2,355.10	511.23
No English			-3,112.53	1,359.3			-629.24	1,261.4
U.S. Citizen			-86.58	281.43			-220.01	261.67
Imm 85-90			-8,164.78	473.96			-6,010.38	440.53
Imm 75-84			-3,711.87	363.92			-3,249.22	338.69
Imm 65-74			-773.21	341.99			-1,060.61	317.43
Child under 6			-8.41	571.24			558.71	530.31

	(1)		(2)		(3)		(4)	
	coef	SE	coef	SE	coef	SE	coef	SE
Over 65 at home			-4,333.51	365.24			-2,795.59	339.11
Labor Mkt Exp			984.57	29.72			675.31	27.92
Labor Mkt Exp^2			-14.25	0.54			-8.61	0.50
Female			-15,780.00	250.40			-11,012.00	240.59
Married			4,306.73	278.16			3,297.04	258.47
Labor Market Context								
Hours Worked					695.20	8.18	565.34	8.19
Public Sector					-3,212.76	388.12	-4,974.67	375.00
Self Employed					8,017.17	325.92	4,485.78	317.49
New York City					7,159.00	401.09	6,198.37	387.29
Los Angeles					4,511.70	419.25	4,309.37	402.33
Filipino Industry					802.47	477.00	2,658.12	461.50
SEI					536.88	5.76	397.28	6.64
R^2	0.01		0.21		0.26		0.32	
N	61,200							

Table 4.15: OLS Regression of Occupational Status Attainment for Filipino Immigrants

	MODEL 1		MODEL 2		MODEL 3		MODEL 4	
	Coef.	S.E.	Coef.	S.E.	Coef.	S.E.	Coef.	S.E.
Intercept	51.90	0.09	25.92	0.48	44.47	0.34	24.07	0.55
Ethnic Background								
FILIPINO	0.67	0.22	-3.36	0.20	-15.46	0.56	-12.72	0.47
Human/Social Capital								
Education			1.79	0.03			1.71	0.03
BA			11.19	0.21			10.72	0.21
English Not Well			-5.11	0.31			-4.66	0.31
No English			-3.33	0.78			-2.83	0.77
U.S. Citizen			0.80	0.16			0.80	0.16
Imm 85-90			-4.16	0.27			-3.89	0.27
Imm 75-84			-2.35	0.21			-2.43	0.21
Imm 65-74			-0.84	0.20			-0.88	0.19
Child under 6			1.40	0.33			1.30	0.32

	Model 1		Model 2		Model 3	
Over 65 at home	-1.31	0.21			-1.11	0.21
Labor Mkt Exp	0.00	0.02			-0.07	0.02
Labor Mkt Exp^2	0.00	0.00			0.00	0.00
Female	-2.25	0.14			-1.91	0.15
Married	1.11	0.16			1.03	0.16
Labor Market Context						
Hours Worked			0.20	0.01	0.09	0.00
Public Sector			8.65	0.27	3.86	0.23
Self Employed			3.93	0.23	2.26	0.19
New York City			-3.02	0.28	-1.33	0.24
Los Angeles			-0.14	0.29	0.16	0.24
Filipino Industry			10.05	0.33	5.96	0.28
R^2	0.340		0.060		0.350	
N	61,200					

likely than foreign-born non-Hispanic whites to work in the public sector and in Filipino industries and less likely to reside in New York City, they maintain an occupational status advantage. If foreign-born non-Hispanic whites were placed in positions similar to the Filipino workers, the gap in occupational status would increase and the sign of the ethnic coefficient would be reversed. In Model 4, FILIPINO remains negative and significant. If human and social capital and labor market context variables were held constant, the occupational status gap would become larger. These data show that Filipino immigrants would lose their occupational status advantage if they had similar human capital and local labor market positions as foreign-born non-Hispanic whites. This is consistent with an argument in which foreign-born non-Hispanic whites are the targets of discrimination, but could also be explained by the effect of other unmeasured variables.

Korean Immigrants

In Table 4.16 I report personal earnings parameter estimates for Korean immigrants and the comparison group. In Model 1, KOREAN has a negative and significant effect on personal earnings. Korean immigrants have lower personal earnings (-$6,682) relative to the white ethnic workers in this sample. After controlling for human and social capital effects in Model 2, the effect of Korean ethnicity remains negative and significant, but becomes 43% smaller. Human and social capital factors ameliorate the effects of Korean ethnicity compared to foreign-born non-Hispanic whites. Korean immigrants are more likely to be recent immigrants and to have lower levels of English language facility than the comparison group, which adversely affects Korean personal earnings. Without those ethnic differences in skills and resources, Koreans would earn relatively more compared to foreign-born non-Hispanic whites.

Model 3 includes the effects of the city level regressors. Between Model 1 and Model 3, the size of the Korean ethnicity coefficient increases by 1.6%, and the sign remains negative. Working in either Immigrant Metropolis city, being self employed, and occupational prestige all have positive and significant effects on earnings. Working in a Korean concentrated industry, which disproportionately affects Korean immigrants, has a negative effect on earnings.

In the final model, KOREAN is reduced by 36% ($2,377) compared to Model 1. More than one third of the covariation between KOREAN and EARN can be explained by ethnic differences in human capital and local labor market indicators. The earnings gap between Korean immigrants and foreign-born non-Hispanic whites would be narrowed if they had similar human and social capital and local labor market conditions. However, even after controlling for these factors, an ethnic residual remains. These findings are consistent with the effect of discrimination, but could also be due to the effect of other unmeasured variables.

As shown in Model 1 in Table 4.17, KOREAN has a negative and significant effect on occupational status. Korean workers have jobs with lower status than foreign-born non-Hispanic whites. Controlling for the effects of human and social capital in Model 2 reduces the size of the Korean ethnicity variable by 26%. Education and marital status have positive and significant effects on SEI, while recent immigration, low levels of English language facility, and being female are negative and significant. Because Koreans in this sample are more likely than the comparison group to be recent immigrants, to have English language deficits, and to be female, this adversely affects their occupational status attainment. Accounting for ethnic differences in human and social capital factors would decrease the status gap between Korean workers and foreign-born non-Hispanic whites by approximately 26%.

In Model 3, KOREAN is positive and significant. Between Model 1 and Model 3, the coefficient increases 260%. Working in Los Angeles has a positive and significant effect on SEI, while working in a Korean concentrated industry has a negative and significant effect. Equating Korean immigrants and foreign-born non-Hispanic whites in terms of local market conditions would reverse the pattern and increase the size of ethnic differences in occupational status. In the final model, KOREAN is positive and statistically significant. Between Model 1 and Model 4, the size of the ethnic heritage coefficient increases by 215%. After controlling for both human and social capital factors and local labor market variables Korean immigrants would be advantaged in terms of job status as compared to foreign-born non-Hispanic whites.

Table 4.16: OLS Regression of Personal Earnings for Korean Immigrants

	MODEL 1		MODEL 2		MODEL 3		MODEL 4	
	Coef.	S.E.	Coef.	S.E.	Coef.	S.E.	Coef.	S.E.
Intercept	32,176.00	148.92	59.04	880.89	-28,629.00	578.11	-34,329.00	963.19
Ethnic Background								
KOREAN	-6,681.61	439.71	-3,824.52	424.30	-6,788.19	684.88	-4,304.95	668.84
Human/Social Capital								
Education			1,668.32	52.15			994.80	50.55
BA			8,684.34	401.83			3,316.63	385.18
English Not Well			-5,654.54	490.09			-3,763.95	460.92
No English			-3,148.89	1,191.09			-870.74	1,114.7
U.S. Citizen			266.10	301.17			149.72	282.50
Imm 85-90			-7,209.73	508.00			-5,358.26	475.95
Imm 75-84			-3,199.65	387.34			-3,104.11	363.53
Imm 65-74			-211.93	364.00			-375.80	340.91
Child under 6			-851.99	646.78			267.82	605.51

	Model 1		Model 2		Model 3		Model 4	
	coef	SE	coef	SE	coef	SE	coef	SE
Over 65 at home			-4,476.06	405.13			-3,180.94	379.31
Labor Mkt Exp			1,081.23	32.01			750.24	30.37
Labor Mkt Exp^2			-15.46	0.57			-9.52	0.54
Female			-16,963.00	268.84			-11,652.00	260.01
Married			4,500.09	300.80			3,513.88	282.12
Labor Market Context								
Hours Worked					665.77	8.37	531.18	8.39
Public Sector					-4,281.04	445.08	-5,718.01	429.45
Self Employed					7,576.01	325.16	3,756.52	317.48
New York City					6,812.39	418.59	5,822.94	403.60
Los Angeles					4,961.15	437.70	4,852.10	419.47
Korean Industry					-720.58	450.10	-381.03	431.60
SEI					547.25	6.21	394.64	7.18
R^2	0.00		0.21		0.24		0.31	
N	57,816							

Table 4.17: OLS Regression of Occupational Status Attainment for Korean Immigrants

	MODEL 1		MODEL 2		MODEL 3		MODEL 4	
	Coef.	S.E.	Coef.	S.E.	Coef.	S.E.	Coef.	S.E.
Intercept	51.90	0.09	26.36	0.48	45.09	0.34	24.11	0.55
Ethnic Background								
KOREAN	-2.69	0.26	-1.98	0.23	4.32	0.46	3.14	0.39
Human/Social Capital								
Education			1.77	0.03			1.70	0.03
BA			10.87	0.22			10.58	0.22
English Not Well			-5.07	0.27			-4.57	0.27
No English			-3.92	0.65			-3.57	0.65
U.S. Citizen			0.66	0.16			0.67	0.16
Imm 85-90			-3.35	0.28			-2.92	0.28
Imm 75-84			-1.98	0.21			-2.05	0.21
Imm 65-74			-1.35	0.20			-1.27	0.20

	Model 1		Model 2		Model 3		Model 4	
Child under 6			1.31	0.35			1.46	0.35
Over 65 at home			-1.04	0.22			-0.89	0.22
Labor Mkt Exp			0.01	0.02			-0.04	0.02
Labor Mkt Exp^2			0.00	0.00			0.00	0.00
Female			-2.69	0.15			-2.06	0.15
Married			0.88	0.16			0.87	0.16
Labor Market Context								
Hours Worked					0.18	0.01	0.08	0.00
Public Sector					10.07	0.30	4.55	0.25
Self Employed					3.54	0.22	1.83	0.18
New York City					-3.29	0.28	-1.45	0.23
Los Angeles					0.66	0.29	0.64	0.24
Korean Industry					-6.69	0.30	-4.75	0.25
R^2	0.002		0.339		0.056		0.353	
N	57,816							

Mexican Immigrants

The effect of Mexican ethnicity on personal earnings is negative and significant as shown in Table 4.18 in Model 1. This earnings gap is 80% ($12,167) larger than the next largest difference between any target ethnic group and the comparison group. Foreign-born non-Hispanic white workers earn substantially more than Mexican immigrants earn. The individual level characteristics in Model 2 improve the fit of the model and reduce the size of MEXICAN to –$6,929. Sixty-three percent of the differences in individual earnings can be attributed to ethnic differences human and social capital between these two groups. However, even after accounting for these differences, Mexican workers are still disadvantaged as compared to foreign-born non-Hispanic whites. Immigrating after 1965, low levels of English language facility, having a family member over age 65, or being female have negative and significant effects on personal earnings. Education, labor market experience, and married status have positive and significant effects. Because Mexican immigrants are more likely than foreign-born non-Hispanic whites to be recent immigrants, to have English language deficits, and to have lower levels of education, they are disadvantaged in terms of personal earnings.

The size of the Mexican coefficient decreases to –$9,609 in Model 3. Between Model 1 and Model 3, 49% of the difference in earnings between Mexican immigrants and the standard group canbe attributed to ethnic differences in local labor market characteristics. If Mexican immigrants shared similar advantageous positions in the labor market with the comparison group, the gap in earnings would be cut in half. For these immigrants, living in either New York City or Los Angeles has a positive and significant effect on earnings, as does being self-employed or working in a Mexican concentrated industry. In Model 4, the size of the Mexican ethnicity coefficient decreases to –$4,979. Between Model 1 and Model 4, 74% of the difference in personal earnings can be attributed to differences in individual skills and resources and job characteristics. Mexican immigrants are more likely to have lower human capital investments, greater social capital deficits, and inferior local labor market placements compared to foreign-born non-Hispanic whites, which adversely affects Mexican personal earnings. If Mexican workers had human capital investments and local labor market conditions similar to the standard group, the gap in personal earnings would be closed substantially. However, even after accounting for differences in human and social capital and for differences in the local market conditions of work, Mexican immigrants still would earn less than foreign-born non-Hispanic whites.

Model 1 in Table 4.19 examines the effect of Mexican ethnic background on occupational status attainment. MEXICAN has a large negative and significant effect on SEI, which parallels the findings in the earnings model. Mexican immigrants hold jobs with the lowest occupational status of all the immigrant groups in this sample. The occupational status difference in Model 1 is almost 18 SEI points. The addition of the human and social capital variables in Model 2 improves the overall fit of the model and changes the Mexican coefficient from approximately –18.0 to –6.2. Ethnic differences in the individual level variables account for 66% of the covariation between Mexican ethnicity and SEI. Education and labor market experience are positive and significant. Low levels of language facility, recent immigration, and being female are negative and significant. These human capital deficits limit Mexican occupational status attainment.

Between Model 1 and Model 3, the size of the Mexican ethnicity effect decreases 26%, but the sign of the ethnic heritage coefficient remains negative. Living in New York City, in Los Angeles, or working in a Mexican concentrated industry have a negative and significant effect on SEI. Given the greater likelihood of Mexican immigrants to live in Los Angeles and to work in a Mexican concentrated industry, this adversely affects their occupational status attainment. In Model 4, 78% percent of the covariation between ethnic background and occupational status can be explained by differences in human and social capital and local labor market conditions. Even after accounting for city level regressors and differences in human and social capital in Model 4, the effect of Mexican ethnicity on SEI is negative and significant. Controlling for differences in skills, resources, and job location reduces, but does not eliminate, the gap in occupational status between Mexican and foreign-born non-Hispanic workers.

Table 4.18: OLS Regression of Personal Earnings for Mexican Immigrants

	MODEL 1		MODEL 2		MODEL 3		MODEL 4	
	Coef.	S.E.	Coef.	S.E.	Coef.	S.E.	Coef.	S.E.
Intercept	32,176.00	114.24	8,742.72	527.97	-19,586.00	404.71	-23,362.00	608.15
Ethnic Background								
MEXICAN	-18,849.00	163.06	-6,929.20	202.07	-9,609.05	299.60	-4,979.21	302.61
Human/Social Capital								
Education			1,039.72	25.03			709.02	23.85
BA			12,366.00	256.06			5,900.01	253.55
English Not Well			-3,377.50	221.15			-1,897.17	208.67
No English			-3,066.03	299.41			-1,140.48	281.53
U.S. Citizen			329.89	181.52			226.21	170.59
Imm 85-90			-6,608.25	300.32			-4,645.26	282.50
Imm 75-84			-4,024.26	246.98			-3,377.78	232.34
Imm 65-74			-1,814.16	235.17			-1,647.14	220.66
Child under 6			1,452.58	338.55			1,499.06	317.24

	b	SE	b	SE	b	SE	b	SE
Over 65 at home			-3,440.13	265.98			-2,613.07	249.37
Labor Mkt Exp			946.20	19.40			677.83	18.38
Labor Mkt Exp^2			-13.99	0.35			-9.17	0.33
Female			-12,630.00	167.53			-8,981.13	160.64
Married			2,845.27	171.45			2,258.06	160.83
Labor Market Context								
Hours Worked					513.40	5.06	415.11	5.01
Public Sector					-2,913.83	293.63	-4,371.32	283.99
Self Employed					6,968.43	233.82	4,378.50	226.32
New York City					6,315.70	309.37	5,523.58	297.05
Los Angeles					4,410.02	312.15	4,297.81	298.99
Mexican Industry					1,298.27	145.31	944.04	140.19
SEI					496.30	4.39	353.65	4.89
R^2	0.12		0.28		0.31		0.37	
N	100,527							

Table 4.19: OLS Regression of Occupational Status Attainment for Mexican Immigrants

	MODEL 1		MODEL 2		MODEL 3		MODEL 4	
	Coef.	S.E.	Coef.	S.E.	Coef.	S.E.	Coef.	S.E.
Intercept	51.90	0.07	35.91	0.32	47.56	0.25	35.40	0.38
Ethnic Background								
MEXICAN	17.97	0.11	-6.24	0.12	-13.25	0.21	-3.94	0.19
Human/Social Capital								
Education			0.85	0.02			0.78	0.02
BA			16.60	0.16			16.26	0.16
English Not Well			-4.07	0.14			-3.51	0.13
No English			-3.45	0.18			-2.86	0.18
U.S. Citizen			0.75	0.11			0.76	0.11
Imm 85-90			-4.03	0.18			-3.48	0.18
Imm 75-84			-2.96	0.15			-2.73	0.15
Imm 65-74			-1.89	0.14			-1.75	0.14
Child under 6			0.57	0.21			0.57	0.20

	Model 1		Model 2		Model 3	
Over 65 at home	-0.25	0.16			-0.10	0.16
Labor Mkt Exp	0.16	0.01			0.13	0.01
Labor Mkt Exp^2	0.00	0.00			0.00	0.00
Female	-2.17	0.10			-1.93	0.10
Married	0.46	0.10			0.48	0.10
Labor Market Context						
Hours Worked			0.13	0.00	0.06	0.00
Public Sector			9.42	0.21	4.48	0.18
Self Employed			4.00	0.17	2.60	0.15
New York City			-3.96	0.22	-2.66	0.19
Los Angeles			-0.49	0.22	-0.14	0.19
Mexican Industry			-3.55	0.10	-2.52	0.09
R^2	0.44		0.27		0.46	
N	100,527					

SUMMARY

In sum, I find small but persistent effects of ethnic heritage on personal earnings and occupational status attainment; however, the direct effect of ethnic heritage is weak. I find strong support for both human and social capital and local labor market arguments. Each of the five target ethnic groups would have lower or equal earnings than foreign-born non-Hispanic whites even if differences in human and social capital and local labor market conditions were eliminated. Human capital and local labor market factors reduce but do not eliminate ethnic differences in personal earnings. The data for the SEI models show that only two target ethnic groups, Filipinos and Mexicans, would have jobs with lower occupational status than the comparison group, if differences in human capital and local labor market factors were eliminated. I will discuss the implications of these findings in Chapter 5.

CHAPTER 5:
Origins and Destinies

In the 1990s, considerable social and economic differences continue to exist between racial and ethnic groups. The projected increase of immigration in the next century makes the overall future of racial and ethnic stratification even more uncertain. The size and nature of contemporary immigration create an opportunity to study this emerging racial and ethnic stratification within the foreign-born community. Examining how ethnic differences in human capital and local labor market conditions affect immigrant assimilation provides a means to assess the persistence ethnic inequality. In this study, I find that ethnic heritage, as well as ethnic variation in human and social capital and local labor market conditions, contributes to differences in immigrant attainment.

INTERPRETATION AND DISCUSSION

The central task of this book assesses the role of ethnic heritage in income and status attainment processes. The basic data show high levels of ethnic variation in socio-economic attainment between the six immigrant groups in this study. My analyses are consistent with the claim that human capital and local labor market placements explain some of the ethnic differences in social and economic attainments. However, my analysis do not permit me to dismiss discrimination as a factor that gives foreign-born non- Hispanic whites direct earnings and occupational status advantages. There is a small but persistent effect of ethnic heritage on earnings and SEI. Although ethnic heritage has a sizeable negative effect on earnings for every target ethnic group as compared to foreign-born non-Hispanic whites, it does not explain a significant portion of the variance in earnings as indicated by the small R^2 in Model 1. The largest ethnic difference in personal earnings is between Mexican workers and foreign-born non-Hispanic whites ($18,849). It is three times larger than the smallest initial difference between Korean immigrants and foreign-born non-Hispanic whites ($6,682). This finding reflects two hierarchies. The first is between foreign-born non-Hispanic whites and the target immigrant groups in this study. White ethnics earn more than the non-white ethnics in this sample do in every case. Second, Asian immigrants earn more than the Hispanic immigrants in this sample. The ethnic background coefficients for the Asian groups are not as large or negative as they are for the Hispanic groups. Economic stratification between the newest immigrant groups is sizeable in terms of the substantive difference in personal earnings.

The models that examine status attainment are similar. I find that for each pair-wise comparison, the fit of Model 1 is poor as indicated by the small R^2. Four of the five target ethnic groups have jobs with lower occupational status than foreign-born non-Hispanic whites. Filipino immigrants have an edge of less than one SEI point over foreign-born non-Hispanic whites; the remaining groups have deficits, which range from approximately –1.6 points (Chinese) to –18 (Mexican). Compared to foreign-born non-Hispanic whites, the Hispanic immigrants have the largest differences in occupational status attributed solely to ethnic background. This finding parallels those on earnings differences. I find an ethnic hierarchy with respect to occupational status that roughly corresponds to the earnings hierarchy.

In Model 2, I estimate the effects of human and social capital in social and economic attainment. The change in the R^2 value from Model 1 to Model 2 indicates that human and social capital explain more of the total variation in earnings and occupational status attainment than ethnic heritage alone. These findings are consistent with the human capital argument. Furthermore, I find that controlling for ethnic differences in skills and resources diminishes the ethnic effect on personal earnings for each target immigrant group. In general, the measured human and social capital variables have significant effects on earnings as Hypothesis 2 predicts. The smallest percentage reduction (13%) in the pair-wise earnings differences is between Filipino immigrants and foreign-born non-Hispanic whites. In contrast, the gap in earnings between Mexican immigrants and the comparison group closes 63% ($11,920) after controlling for these differences. Equating the target ethnic groups and foreign-born non-Hispanic whites in terms of human capital reduces, but does not eliminate, differences in earnings. All of the target immigrant groups would still have substantially lower earnings than foreign-born non-Hispanic whites even after ethnic differences in human and social capital were eliminated.

Ethnic differences in human and social capital account for some of the variation in occupational status as well. Every ethnic group except Filipinos would have higher job status if differences in skills and resources were eliminated. In fact, Chinese immigrants would surpass the comparison group by 0.7 SEI points. Despite the reduction in ethnic differences in occupational status after human and social capital are accounted for, four of the five target ethnic groups would still have lower SEI scores than foreign-born non-Hispanic whites.

In Model 3, I control for ethnic differences in local labor market conditions. I find strong support for the local labor market arguments as evidenced by the substantial increase in R^2 from Model 1 to Model 3. Differences in local labor market characteristics explain a sizeable portion of the variance in personal earnings. The measured local labor market variables have the expected effects on earnings as Hypotheses 3 and 4 predict. Furthermore, the addition of these variables reduces the strength of the ethnic effect for four of the five target ethnic groups. For every group except Korean immigrants, I find a substantial reduction in the size of the ethnic effect once differences in local labor market conditions are eliminated. Once I account for ethnic differences in these factors, the gap in earnings is reduced by nearly half for Mexican and Chinese immigrants. The Korean ethnic background parameter actually increases in size by $106 (1.6%) in Model 3. Given that Korean immigrants are almost twice as likely to be self-employed than the comparison group, they have more advantageous local labor market positions. If a greater number of foreign-born non-Hispanic whites were self-employed, the gap in earnings between these two groups would actually increase. Moreover, even if all six groups were equated in terms of their placement in local labor markets, the target ethnic groups would still earn substantially less than foreign-born non-Hispanic whites.

Eliminating differences in local labor market conditions would reduce or eliminate the occupational status gap between foreign-born non-Hispanic whites and the five target ethnic groups. Chinese, Korean, and Cuban immigrants would all have SEI scores higher than foreign-born non-Hispanic whites once differences in job placements were removed. The occupational status gap between the comparison group and Mexican immigrants would close 4.7 points and the gap with Filipino immigrants would close 14.8 points if differences in local labor market conditions were eliminated. Both groups would still rank behind foreign-born non-Hispanic whites in terms of occupational status.

In the full model, the effect of ethnic background on economic attainment is considerably smaller as compared to the zero order associations in Model 1. Once I control for differences in human capital and local labor market conditions, there is no statistically significant difference in earnings between Chinese workers and foreign-born non-Hispanic workers. A substantive $1,000 difference between the groups remains, but it falls within the normal income distribution. Although there is a reduction in the size of the ethnic effect for the remaining four groups, they all would earn less than foreign-born non-Hispanic whites *even if differences in the independent variables were eliminated.* The gap in earnings that remains after controlling for both sets of factors for the other four groups ranges from a low of $2,729 for Cuban immigrants to a high of $7,673 for Filipino immigrants. The existence of sizeable, although reduced, residual ethnic background effects for all groups except Chinese immigrants are important. While I cannot claim that the data support the discrimination argument, they suggest that the remaining differences in earnings are due to unmeasured factors, which may include racial and ethnic discrimination. In fact, some of the ethnic differences in human capital and local labor market positions also may be due to discrimination in educational opportunities and employment practices.

Eliminating ethnic differences in both human and social capital and local labor market conditions would decrease the gap in occupational status for all of the target immigrant groups except Filipinos. Chinese, Korean, and Cuban immigrants would have higher occupational status than the control group. Although the gap between foreign-born non-Hispanic whites and Mexican immigrants would close by 14 SEI points, it would not be eliminated. Filipino immigrants would become disadvantaged with respect to the comparison group if differences in human capital and local labor market conditions were eliminated.

In sum, foreign-born non-Hispanic whites have an advantage in earnings and occupational status attainment compared to the five target immigrant groups in this study. Although I find that human capital and local labor market conditions explain part of the ethnic differences in social and economic attainment, my analyses do not permit me to rule out discrimination as a factor that gives foreign-born non-Hispanic whites direct earnings and occupational status advantages.

The similarity of disadvantageous results for the five target immigrant groups should not mask the magnitude of differences that exist across the Asian and Hispanic groups or within each subgroup. Except for the Chinese immigrants, the non-white income disadvantage is not eliminated when human and social capital and local labor market characteristics are taken into account. Social capital deficits offset the educational advantages that Chinese immigrants have. They report greater difficulty with English language facility and a shorter time since immigration than foreign-born non-Hispanic whites, both of which may lower Chinese earnings.

The other target ethnic groups remain disadvantaged in terms of personal earnings even after differences in human capital and local labor market placement are eliminated as evidenced by the residual ethnic heritage effect in Model 4. Mexican immigrants are the youngest, least formally educated, and most recent immigrants to arrive in the U.S., which may leave them disadvantaged as compared to foreign-born non-Hispanic whites and the other immigrant groups in this sample. Their legal status and the tendency for them to find work in the agricultural sector may leave them vulnerable to low wage and low status positions. The data for Cuban immigrants are similar to the Mexican attainment models. The difference in earnings between foreign-born non-Hispanic whites and Cuban immigrants would close substantially if they were equated in terms of human capital and local labor market characteristics. However, an earnings gap between the two groups would remain. The greater likelihood of Cuban immigrants to work in Miami, the densest concentration of Cuban immigrants in the U.S., may depress Cuban personal earnings as compared to foreign-born non-Hispanic whites.

Filipino and Korean immigrants share relatively high educational attainment as compared to foreign-born non-Hispanic whites. However, their human capital investments are offset by other factors. Almost one third of the Korean immigrants in this sample are entrepreneurs. Instead of working in the open and more formal segments of the economy, Korean immigrants may use prior investments in human capital to open small businesses. Alternatively, they may be limited to this economic niche by employer discrimination. As a group, this niche improves their income attainment, since being self-employed raises individual earnings by $7,500, yet their earnings are lower than the comparison group. A greater proportion of recent immigrants and lower English language facility may offset the human capital and local labor market advantages Koreans have as compared to foreign-born non-Hispanic whites. The gap in earnings between Filipino immigrants and the comparison group actually increases after human capital and local labor market conditions are taken into account. A greater proportion female and more recent immigration than the comparison group offset educational advantages for Filipino immigrants. Filipino immigrants also are more likely to find positions within the public sector that may have relatively high status but lower pay as compared to foreign-born non-Hispanic whites.

The status attainment models have more mixed results than the earnings models. Filipino and Mexican immigrants would remain disadvantaged relative to the comparison group even after differences in human capital and local labor market characteristics were eliminated. However, foreign-born non-Hispanic whites would be disadvantaged relative to Chinese, Cuban, and Korean immigrants controlling for these same factors. I find considerable support for both the human capital and the local labor market arguments in these findings. The existence of residual significant differences suggests that some of the effects of ethnic heritage are due to other unmeasured variables and possibly racial and ethnic discrimination. The disadvantage that remains for Filipino and Mexican immigrants is consistent with the idea that white ethnics have advantages that non-white ethnics do not. However, the SEI data for the other three groups suggests a more complicated process, especially given their lower earnings. These particular three groups may show an SEI advantage, but not an earnings advantage, because of their position in local labor markets. These groups would be able to attain higher status jobs if they weren't impeded by their local labor market positions. My data does not dismiss the possibility that employer discrimination limits the local labor market positions of contemporary immigrants.

ALTERNATIVE EXPLANATIONS

One of the major tasks of this book has been to unify diverse literatures on immigrant assimilation and attainment. Although I do not specifically test other social and economic attainment models, the data are relevant to arguments other than the ones I describe. Support for these alternative arguments underscores the complexity of immigrant attainment processes.

Ethnic Enclave

Ethnic enclaves may reduce some of the costs to working in an unfamiliar cultural and linguistic environment because ethnic workers may be able to use human capital investments by working for an ethnic boss or starting an ethnic enterprise. To that end, immigrants may fare better economically and socially within the bounds of the enclave. Although I do not specifically test for the presence of an ethnic enclave, I do include a variable that indicates working in an ethnic industry.

Controlling for the other independent variables, a local labor market placement in an ethnic industry would have a positive effect on earnings and occupational status for groups that benefit from working in an ethnic economy. My data show that working in an ethnic industry has a negative effect on Chinese earnings, a positive effect on Mexican earnings, and no statistically significant effect for the other three target ethnic groups. For the occupational status attainment models, there is a positive effect for Filipino workers and a negative effect for the other four groups for working in an ethnic industry. For Mexican workers, there is a substantial benefit to working in an ethnic labor market. Working in a Mexican concentrated industry helps narrow the earnings difference with the comparison group, net of other factors. Eliminating differences in labor market placements between the target ethnic group and foreign-born non-Hispanic whites would actually hurt Mexican immigrants in terms of personal earnings because of their advantageous ethnic labor market placements, net of human capital investments.

In contrast, Chinese immigrants are actually disadvantaged by working in an ethnic industry. For this group, working in a Chinese industry has a negative effect on earnings, net of the other independent variables. Although the enclave may be a protected economic arena for some immigrants, the gap between Chinese and foreign-born non-Hispanic white workers would decrease if Chinese immigrants had more advantageous labor market placements. The occupational status models support this finding as well. In general, working in an ethnic industry has negative effects on SEI. Workers may have jobs in ethnic industries, but their occupational status is limited by this labor market placement. In general, ethnic industries hurt the occupational status of non-white groups in this sample, but the effects on earnings vary by ethnic group.

Model Minority

The model minority argument implies that the cultural systems of certain ethnic groups stress particular values, attitudes, and ethics that promote the acquisition of skills that ensure greater success for its members than for other ethnic groups. If they were model minorities, the superior human capital investments of the Asian immigrants in this study would leave them poised to take advantage of high paying job opportunities in the U.S. not available to the Hispanic groups or foreign-born non-Hispanic whites. My data show that the three Asian immigrant groups have higher educational credentials and levels of English language facility than either of the Hispanic groups. Moreover, the Korean and Filipino immigrants surpass foreign-born non-Hispanic whites in terms of educational attainment. Education does enhance earnings and job status, but in this sample, these human capital investments are often offset by other factors. Only Korean immigrants have personal earnings that are similar to the comparison group. Filipino immigrants, who have the highest educational credentials, are the third highest earners behind the comparison group and Korean immigrants. For the other groups, ethnic differences in educational attainment increase the earnings gap, which range from $443 for Chinese immigrants to $5,096 for Mexican immigrants.

I find some support for the model minority argument in the Filipino occupational status scores. Filipino immigrants have jobs with slightly higher SEI scores than do foreign-born non-Hispanic whites. In this case, the group with the highest educational credentials also has the highest occupational status scores. The other four target ethnic groups fall behind the comparison group with respect to occupational status attainment. For the most part, ethnic differences in human capital factors and local labor market positions increase the gap in earnings and occupational status with foreign-born non-Hispanic whites. This may result from lower investments or poorer labor market positions overall, but may also be attributed to unmeasured factors, including discrimination. Their lower educational investments increase the occupational status gap by 3.8 SEI points for Chinese immigrants to a high of 15.9 SEI points for Mexican immigrants. The public impression of Asian immigrants as model minorities is not substantiated in my analyses. Overall, my data suggest that the model minority in this sample is foreign-born non-Hispanic whites because they have high levels of education, personal earnings, and relatively high status jobs.

CONCLUSION

In this book, I examine the relationship between ethnic background and social and economic attainment. I consider how ethnic differences in human and social capital and in local labor market conditions affect the association between ethnic heritage and attainment. I find a small and consistent direct effect of ethnic heritage on earning and status attainment. Controlling for differences in human and social capital and local labor market conditions, reduces, but does not eliminate, the earnings advantage white ethnics have over the Asian and Hispanic immigrants in this study. My data do not permit me to dismiss discrimination as a factor that gives foreign-born non-Hispanic whites both a direct and indirect earnings advantage.

The non-white immigrant groups in the sample fare better with respect to SEI. Ethnic differences in human and social capital and local labor market conditions explain the gap in SEI scores for three of the five target ethnic groups. Only Mexican and Filipino immigrants would have an occupational status gap with foreign-born non-Hispanic whites after human capital and local labor market differences were eliminated.

My findings suggest that ethnic inequality on many social and economic dimensions will persist well into the 21st century. The rapid assimilation of some foreign-born groups compared to the difficulties others have in reaching social and economic parity with native-born groups raises questions about the nature of contemporary immigrant attainment. Ethnic variation in human and social capital leaves some groups poised to fare well and limits the attainment of others. Differences in local labor market placements can also facilitate or impede assimilation. Some groups are unable to reach high levels of attainment, which may be due to the effects of discrimination in the earnings and occupational status processes, educational opportunities, and/or employment practices.

Due to the changes in origins of immigrants and in the economic climate of the U.S. economy, contemporary immigrant attainment does not follow the same path as it did at the turn of the century. Today, there are several modes of attainment for the varied cultural, ethnic, and racial groups who immigrate to the U.S. Inferences about the future of the six groups in this sample speak to the health of racial and ethnic relations in general. I expect differences in earnings and in occupational status attainment between foreign-born non-Hispanic whites and Chinese and Korean immigrants to narrow as these groups proceed over the lifecourse due to similarities in their human capital investments. The next generation might be essentially similar to the children of foreign-born non-Hispanic whites and follow traditional assimilation pathways as we have seen in the past. As Filipino immigrants augment their investments in human capital with labor market experience in the U.S., I expect their social and economic attainment to improve. Once this group has accumulated sufficient experience within local labor markets, I expect them to find better paying and higher status jobs in the private sector. As the second generation of Cuban immigrants invests in education and training outside the Miami economy, I expect this group, as well, to narrow the earnings gap with the white immigrant groups. For these groups, immigrant assimilation may happen over the course of a generation. In contrast, Mexican immigrants may remain disadvantaged compared to the other ethnic groups in this study and foreign-born non-Hispanic whites. The continual large-scale movement of legal and illegal Mexican immigrants across the U.S. border maintains a supply of unskilled labor that limits their earnings as a group. In short, ethnic stratification among contemporary immigrant groups will continue. For most groups, investments in human capital will reduce the gap in social and economic attainment and improved local labor market positions will offset other deficits.

In short, my research suggests that racial and ethnic stratification will persist into the next century. The income attainments of first generation Asian and Hispanic immigrants are substantially lower than those of the foreign-born non-Hispanic whites in my sample. Non-white immigrants also tend to have lower status occupation than white immigrants. Improved investments in human and social capital factors will enhance the lifechances of non-white immigrants and their children. Their earnings and occupational status will also improve as they become more integrated into local labor markets. However, the most telling finding of this research concerns the marked ethnic differences in earnings that remain after I account for the effects of human and social capital and local labor market placements. While I cannot attribute all of these residual effects to ethnic discrimination, their existence certainly is consistent with discrimination arguments. Whether non-white immigrants and their descendants eventually attain parity with foreign-born non-Hispanic whites, or native-born groups for that matter, may ultimately depend on our nation's ability to eliminate the last vestiges of racial and ethnic discrimination from the fabric of American life.

Bibliography

Alba, Richard D. 1989. "The Twilight of Ethnicity Among Americans of European Ancestry: The Case of Italians." pp. 134-158 in *Ethnicity and Race in the USA: Toward the Twenty-First Century* ed. Richard D. Alba. New York: Routledge & Kegan Paul.

Bailey, Thomas and Roger Waldinger. 1991. "Primary, Secondary, and Enclave Labor Markets: A Training Systems Approach." *American Sociological Review* 56: 432-445.

Baron, James N. and William T. Bielby. 1984. "The Organization of Work in a Segmented Economy." *American Sociological Review* 49: 454-473.

Becker, Gary S. 1957. *The Economics of Discrimination*. Chicago: University of Chicago Press.

Becker, Gary S. 1964. *Human Capital: A Theoretical and Empirical Analysis with Special Reference to Education*. New York: Columbia University Press.

Bendix, Richard and Seymour Martin Lipset. 1966. *Class, Status, and Power* 2ed. New York: Free Press.

Binder, Frederick M., and David M. Reimers. 1996. "New York as an Immigrant City" pp. 334-345 in *Origins and Destinies: Immigration, Race, and Ethnicity in America*, eds Silvia Pedraza and Rubén G. Rumbaut. New York: Wadsworth.

Blau, Peter. 1977. *Cross-cutting Social Circles: Testing a Macrostructural Theory of Intergroup Relations.* Orlando, FL: Academic Press.

Blauner, Robert. 1987. "Colonized and Immigrant Minorities." pp. 149-160 in *From Different Shores: Perspectives on Race and Ethnicity in America* ed. Ronald Takaki. New York: Oxford University Press.

Bonacich, Edna 1972. "A Theory of Ethnic Antagonism: The Split Labor Market." *American Sociological Review* 37: 547-559.

Bonacich, Edna 1973. "A Theory of Middleman Minorities." *American Sociological Review* 38: 583-594.

Bonacich, Edna. 1976. "Advanced Capitalism and Black/White Race Relations in the United States: A Split Labor Market Interpretation." *American Sociological Review* 41: 34-51.

Bourdieu, Pierre. 1984. *Distinction: A Social Critique of the Judgment of Taste,* translated by Richard Nice. Cambridge, MA: Harvard University Press.

Bouvier, Leon F. and Lindsey Grant. 1994. *How Many Americans? Population, Immigration, and the Environment.* San Francisco: Sierra Club Books.

Bozorgmehr, Mehdi, Georges Sabagh, and Ivan Light. 1996. "Los Angeles: Explosive Diversity." pp. 346-359 in *Origins and Destinies: Immigration, Race, and Ethnicity in America* eds Silvia Pedraza and Rubén G. Rumbaut. New York: Wadsworth.

Brimelow, Peter. (1995). *Alien Nation: Common Sense About America's Immigration Disaster.* New York: Random House.

Briggs, Vernon Jr. and Stephen Moore 1994. *Still an Open Door? U.S. Immigration Policy and the American Economy.* Washington, D.C.: The American University Press

Brown, W.O. 1934. "Culture Contact and Race Conflict" in E.B. Reuter ed, *Race and Culture Contact*. *New York: McGraw Hill Press*.

Chiswick, Barry R. 1982. "The Employment of Immigrants in the United States." *Contemporary Economic Problems*. Washington D.C.: American Enterprise Institute.

Chiswick, Barry R. 1986. "Mexican Immigrants: The Economic Dimension." *Annals of the American Academy of Political and Social Science* 487:92-101.

Clark, Rebecca L., Jeffrey S. Passel, Wendy N. Zimmermann, and Michael Fix. 1994. *Fiscal Impacts of Undocumented Aliens: Selected Estimates for Seven Cities*. Washington D.C.: Urban Institute Press.

Cohen, Bernard P. 1989. *Developing Sociological Knowledge 2ed*. Chicago: Nelson-Hall.

Coleman, James S. 1988. "Social Capital in the Creation of Human Capital." *American Journal of Sociology* 94:S95-S120.

Crèvecouer, J. Hector St. John de. 1782 [1912]. *Letters From an American Farmer*. New York: E. P. Dutton & Co.

Cummings, Scott. 1983. *Immigrant Minorities and the Working Class*. Port Washington, NY: Associated Faculty Press, Inc.

Daniels, Roger. 1988. *Asian America: Chinese and Japanese in the US Since 1850*. Seattle: University of Washington Press.

Daniels, Roger. 1991. *Coming to America: A History of Immigration and Ethnicity in American Life*. New York: Harper Perennial.

Dodoo, F. Nii-Amoo. (1997). "Assimilation Differences among Africans in America." *Social Forces* 76: 527-546.

Edwards, Richard and Paolo Garonna. 1991. *The Forgotten Link: Labor's Stake in International Economic Cooperation.* Savage, MD: Rowman and Littlefield Publishers, Inc.

Evans, M.D.R. 1989. "Immigrant Entrepreneurship: Effects of Ethnic Market Size and Isolated Labor Pool." *American Sociological Review* 54: 950-962.

Fosler, Scott R, William Alonso, Jack A. Meyer, and Rosemary Kern. 1990. *Demographic Change and the American Future.* Pittsburgh, PA: University of Pittsburgh Press.

Freeman, Richard B. and John M. Abowd. 1990. *Immigration, Trade and the Labor Market.* Chicago: University of Chicago Press.

Gall, Timothy L. 1995. *Worldmark Encyclopedia of the States.* New York: Gale Research Inc.

Gans, Herbert J. 1979. "Symbolic Ethnicity: The Future of Ethnic Groups and Culture in America." *Ethnic and Racial Studies* 2: 1-20.

Gans, Herbert J. 1992. "Second-generation Decline: Scenarios for the Economic and Ethnic Futures of the Post-1965 American Immigrants." *Ethnic and Racial Studies* 15: 173-192.

Glazer, Nathan, and Daniel P. Moynihan. 1963. *Beyond the Melting Pot: The Negroes, Puerto Ricans, Jews, Italians and Irish of New York City.* Cambridge, Mass: M.I.T. Press.

Gordon, Milton M. 1964. *Assimilation in American Life: The Role of Race, Religion, and National Origins.* New York: Oxford University Press.

Granovetter, Mark. 1973. "The Strength of Weak Ties." *American Journal of Sociology* 78: 1360-1380.

Granovetter, Mark. 1985. "Economic Action, Social Structure, and Embeddedness." *American Journal of Sociology* 91:481-510.

Greneir, Guillermo J and Lisandro Pérez. 1996. "Miami Spice: The Ethnic Cauldron Simmers" pp. 360-372 in *Origins and Destinies: Immigration, Race, and Ethnicity in America*, eds. Silvia Pedraza and Rubén G. Rumbaut. New York: Wadsworth.

Handlin, Oscar. 1951. *The Uprooted: The Epic Story of the Great Migration that Made the American People*. Boston: Little Brown.

Hannan, Michael T. 1979. "The Dynamics of Ethnic Boundaries in Modern States" pp. 253-275 in *National Development and the World System* eds. J. Meyer and M.T. Hannan. Chicago: University of Chicago Press.

Hiestand, Dale L. and Dean W. Morse. 1979. *Comparative Metropolitan Employment Complexes: New York, Chicago, Los Angeles, Houston, Atlanta*. New York: Allenheld Osmun and Co. Publishers Inc.

Hirschman, Charles O. 1983. "America's Melting Pot Reconsidered." *Annual Review of Sociology* 9:397-423.

Hecter, Michael. 1978. "Group Formation and the Cultural Division of Labor." *American Journal of Sociology* 84: 293-318.

Heer, David M. 1996. *Immigration in America's Future*. Boulder, CO: Westview Press.

Kalmijn, Matthijs. 1996. "The Socioeconomic Assimilation of Caribbean American Blacks." *Social Forces*. 74(4): 911-930.

Keely, Charles B. 1979. *U.S. Immigration: A Policy Analysis*. New York: Population Council.

Lamm, Richard D. and Gary Imhoff. 1985. *The Immigration Time Bomb: The Fragmenting of America*. New York: Truman Talley Books.

Lieberson, Stanley. 1980. *A Piece of the Pie: Blacks and White Immigrants Since 1880.* Berkeley: University of California Press.

Lieberson, Stanley. 1989. "Unhyphenated Whites in the United States." pp. 159-180 in *Ethnicity and Race in the USA: Toward the Twenty-First Century* ed. Richard D. Alba. New York: Routledge and Kegan Paul.

Lin, Nan. 1982. "Social Resources and Instrumental Action" pp. 131-146 in *Social Structure and Network Analysis* ed. by P. Marsden and N. Lin. Beverly Hills, CA: Sage.

Lipset, Seymour M. and Stein Rokkan. 1967. "Cleavage, Structure, Party Systems, and Voter Alignments." pp. 1-62 in *Party Systems and Voter Alignments*, eds. S.M. Lipset and S. Rokkan. New York: The Free Press.

Logan, John R., Richard D. Alba, and Thomas L. McNulty. 1994. "Ethnic Economies in Metropolitan Regions: Miami and Beyond." *Social Forces* 72: 691-724.

Loewen, James W. 1988. *The Mississippi Chinese: Between Black and White,* 2nd ed. Prospect Heights, IL: Waveland Press.

Massey, Douglas S. 1986. "The Social Organization of Mexican Migration to the United States" *American Academy of Political and Social Science* 487: 102-113.

Massey, Douglas, Rafael Alarcon, Jorge Durand, and Humberto Gonzales. 1987. *Return to Aztlan: The Social Process of International Migration from Western Mexico.* Los Angeles: University of California Press.

Massey, Douglas, Luin Goldring and Jorge Durand. 1994. "Continuities in Transnational Migration: An Analysis of Nineteen Mexican Communities." *American Journal of Sociology* 99: 1492-1533.

Mincer, Jacob 1993. *Studies in Human Capital: Collected Essays of Jacob Mincer*. Brookfield, VT: Edward Elgar Publishing Limited.

Mosteller, Frederic and John W. Tukey. 1977. *Data Analysis and Regression: A Second Course in Statistics*. Reading, MA: Addison –Wesley Publishing Company.

Mullen, Thomas, and Thomas J. Espenshade. 1985. *The Fourth Wave: California's Newest Immigrants*. Washington, DC: Urban Institute.

Murdock, Steven. 1995. *An America Challenged: Population Change and the Future of the United States*. Boulder, CO: Westview Press.

Nakao, Keiko and Judith Treas. 1994. "Updating Occupational Prestige and Socioeconomic Scores: How the New Measures Measure Up." *Sociological Methodology* 4: 1-72.

Nee, Victor G. and Brett de Bary Nee. 1973. *Longtime Californ': A Documentary Study of an American Chinatown*. New York: Pantheon Books.

Nee, Victor and Jimy Sanders. 1987. "On Testing the Enclave-Economy Hypothesis." *American Sociological Review* 52: 771-773.

Nee, Victor and Jimy Sanders. 1990. "A Theory of Immigrant Incorporation." Department of Sociology, *Cornell University, Technical Report 90-2*.

Nee, Victor, Jimy Sanders and Scott Sernau. 1994 "Job Transitions in an Immigrant Metropolis." *American Sociological Review* 59: 849-872.

North, Douglass. 1993. "Five Propositions on Institutional Change." Unpublished.

North, Douglass C. 1990. *Institutions, Institutional Change, and Economic Performance.* New York: Cambridge University Press.

Noyelle, Thierry J. and Thomas M. Stanback, Jr. 1983. *The Economic Transformation of American Cities.* Totowa, NJ: Rowman and Allenheld, Publishers.

Olzak, Susan. 1983. "Contemporary Ethnic Mobilization." *Annual Review of Sociology* 9: 355-374.

Olzak, Susan. 1986. "A Competition Model of Ethnic Collective Action in American Cities, 1877-1889." In *Competitive Ethnic Relations* eds. Susan Olzak and Joane Nagel, pp. 17-46. New York: Academic Press.

Olzak, Susan. 1989. "Labor Unrest, Immigration, and Ethnic Conflict in Urban America, 1880-1914." *American Journal of Sociology* 94: 1303-1333.

Olzak, Susan. 1990. "The Political Context of Competition: Lynching and Urban Racial Violence 1822-1914." *Social Forces* 69: 395-421.

Park, Robert E. 1950. *Race and Culture.* Glencoe, IL: The Free Press.

Park, Robert E. and Ernest W. Burgess. 1926. *Introduction to the Science of Sociology.* Chicago: University of Chicago Press.

Parsons, Talcott. 1951. *The Social System.* Glencoe, IL: Free Press.

Passel, Jeffrey S. 1986. "Undocumented Immigration." *Annals of the American Academy of Political and Social Science* 487: 181-200.

Perez, Lisandro. 1986. "Cubans in the United States." *Annals of the American Academy of Political and Social Science* 487: 126-137.

Piore, Michael. 1975. "Notes for a Theory of Labor Market Stratification" pp. 125-150 in *Labor Market Segregation,* ed. R.C. Edwards et al. Lexington, MA: Health.

Piore, Michael. 1979. *Birds of Passage: Migrant Labor and Industrial Societies* New York: Cambridge University Press.

Portes, Alejandro. 1984. "The Rise of Ethnicity: Determinants of Ethnic Perception Among Cubans in Miami." *American Sociological Review* 49: 383-397.

Portes, Alejandro and Robert Bach. 1985. *Latin Journey: Cuban and Mexican Immigrants in the United States.* Los Angeles: University of California Press.

Portes, Alejandro and Leif Jensen. 1987. "What's an Ethnic Enclave? The Case for Conceptual Clarity." *American Sociological Review* 52: 768-771.

Portes, Alejandro and Leif Jensen. 1989. "The Enclave and the Entrants: Patterns of Ethnic Enterprise in Miami Before and After Mariel." *American Sociological Review* 54: 929-949.

Portes, Alejandro and Rubén G. Rumbaut. 1996. *Immigrant America: A Portrait.* Los Angeles: University of California Press.

Portes, Alejandro and Julia Sensenbrenner. 1993. "Embeddedness and Immigration: Notes on the Social Determinants of Economic Action. *American Journal of Sociology* 98: 1320-1350.

Portes, Alejandro and Min Zhou. 1992. "Gaining the Upper Hand: Economic Mobility Among Immigrant and Domestic Minorities." *Ethnic and Racial Studies* 15: 491-522.

Ragin, Charles C. 1979. "Ethnic Political Mobilization: The Welsh Case." *American Sociological Review* 44: 619-635.

Reich, Michael, David Gordon, and Richard Edwards. 1973. "Dual Labor Markets: A Theory of Labor Market Segmentation." *American Economic Review* 63: 359-365.

Rokkan, Stein. 1970. *Citizens, Elections, and Parties.* Chicago: Rand McNally.

Ryan, Paul. 1981. "Segmentation and Duality in the Internal Labor Market." pp. 3-20 in *The Dynamics of Labor Market Segmentation* edited by Frank Wilkinson. New York: Academic Press.

Sanders, Jimy and Victor Nee. 1996. "Immigrant Self-Employment: The Family as Social Capital and the Value of Human Capital." *American Sociological Review 61*: 231-249.

Sanders, Jimy M. and Victor Nee. 1987. "Limits of Ethnic Solidarity in the Enclave Economy." *American Sociological Review* 52: 745-767.

SAS/STAT User's Guide version 6, 4th ed. Volumes 1 and 2. 1989. Cary, NC: SAS Institute Inc.

Schlesinger, Arthur M, Jr. 1992. *The Disuniting of America.* W.W. Norton & Company, Inc.

Scott, Allen J. 1985. *Metropolis.* Los Angeles: University of California Press.

Stanback, Thomas M. Jr. and Thierry J. Noyelle. 1982. *Cities in Transition.* Totowa, NJ: Allenheld, Osmun and Co. Publishers Inc.

Turner, Frederick Jackson. 1893 [1920]. *The Frontier in American History.* New York: Holt Rinehart and Winston.

Wacquant, Loic J.D., and William Julius Wilson. 1989. "The Cost of Racial and Class Exclusion in the Inner City" *Annals of the American Academy of Political and Social Science* 501: 8-25.

Waldinger, Roger. 1993. "The Ethnic Enclave Debate Revisited." Department of Sociology, UCLA, *Working Paper Series -249.*

White, Michael J., Ann E. Biddlecom, and Shenyang Guo. 1993. "Immigration, Naturalization, and Residential Assimilation Among Asian Americans." *Social Forces* 72: 93-117.

Wilson, Kenneth L. and Alejandro Portes. 1980. "Immigrant Enclaves: An Analysis of the Labor Market Experiences of Cubans in Miami." *American Journal of Sociology* 86: 295-319.

Wong, Morrison G. 1986. "Post-1965 Asian Immigrants: Where Do They Come From, Where Are They Now, and Where Are They Going?" *Annals of the American Academy of Political and Social Science* 487:150-168.

U.S. Department of Labor, Bureau of International Affairs. 1989. *The Effects of Immigration on the U.S. Economy and Labor Market, Immigration Policy and Research Report 1.* Washington DC: U.S. Government Printing Office.

Yang, Philip Q. 1995 *Post-1965 Immigration to the United States: Structural Determinants.* Westport, CT: Praeger.

Young, Frank W. 1993. "Explanations of Development: A Classification and an Elaboration." Unpublished document.

Index

9 781931 202169